# How to befriend, tame, manage, and teach your Black Dog called Depression using CBT

ACCESSIBLE CBT TECHNIQUES, CBT PRINCIPLES, CBT
WORKSHEETS, AND ONLINE CBT RESOURCES FOR DEPRESSION
IN A NUTSHELL

Written by Dr James Manning

Published by the West Suffolk CBT Service Ltd

Voice of the Black Dog by Dr Nicola Ridgeway & Dr James Manning

# About the author

Dr James Manning is a Consultant Clinical Psychologist and the Managing Director of the West Suffolk CBT Service. James has post-graduate qualifications in both Clinical Psychology and Counselling Psychology. He has regularly offered workshops and training to clinicians throughout the United Kingdom on CBT and continues to work as a therapist.

# By the author

Think About Your Thinking to Stop Depression

How to Help Your Loved One Overcome Depression

The Little Book on CBT for Depression

A Simple Introduction to Cognitive Behaviour Therapy for Visual Learners

CBT Worksheets

CBT: What it is and how it works (2nd Edition)

My CBT Journal

CBT Worksheets for Anxiety

CBT Worksheets for Teenage Social Anxiety

Breaking free from social anxiety

A Journey with Panic

Fused: A memoir of childhood OCD and adult obsession

How to befriend, tame, manage and teach your black dog called depression using CBT

How to befriend, tame, manage, and teach your Black Dog called Depression using CBT (or cognitive Behaviour Therapy): Accessible CBT techniques, CBT principles, CBT worksheets, and online CBT resources for depression in a nutshell

Written by Dr James Manning, ClinPsyD

This edition printed 2016

Edited by Nick Hodgson

Technical advisor, Dr Nicola Ridgeway

# Contents

vii ............................................................................Preface

1 ..................................................................Introduction to the Black Dog

5 ..................................................................How the brain works

10 ...........................................................What encourages the Black Dog to stay?

13 ...........................................................Serotonin and 5HT

18 ...........................................................Getting to know your Black Dog

25 ...........................................................Consider going to a Black Dog expert

30 ...........................................................Making a start using CBT

33 ...........................................................Avoidance and safety behaviours

36 ...........................................................Self-observation

43 ...........................................................Cognitive distortions

47 ...........................................................Rules

59 ...........................................................Limiting beliefs

65 ...........................................................Drawing out simple cycles

70 ...........................................................More cycles

75 ...........................................................How to complete a CBT cycle

79 ...........................................................Challenging negative automatic thoughts

89 ...........................................................Approaching feelings

92 ...........................................................Working with emotions

98 ...........................................................Breaking patterns of rumination

104 ...........................................................Behavioural experiments

109 ...........................................................Using desensitisation

115 ...........................................................Exposure

118 ...........................................................Help with the Black Dog

127 ...........................................................Conclusion

129 ...........................................................Regulatory organisations in the UK

130 ........................................................................ References and additional reading

132 ............................................................................................Glossary

134 ...................................................................................Common medications

135 ...................................................................................................Index

136 ........................................................................ Advice for loved ones

# By Dr James Manning

I am grateful for the freedom that psychological knowledge has given me. It has given me a life I value living and it has offered me an opportunity to help many others along the way. At the risk of sounding a total f\*\*k-up, I'll explain the background to my life. Hopefully, it will give you some kind of an idea about how I developed such a passionate interest in psychology and how I came to write this book.

Between the ages of 15 and 30, I had a visit from a breed of Black Dog, called Dysthymia. Before this, I experienced sensory hyper-sensitivity, excessive avoidance, attention deficit, obsessive compulsive problems, paranoia, and anxiety. In short, during this time I had significant mental health problems.

I knew that I was different from other people at a very young age, as did my family, but I didn't have any explanation for it. As I got older, I attempted to cope with problems that life presented me using food, drugs, gambling, and alcohol. I developed a significant alcohol problem as soon as I looked old enough to buy alcohol from an off-licence, (which was when I was about 17).

In my early life the emotion that I struggled with the most was low mood: I had a feeling of being slowed down, and an emptiness that sapped my motivation to engage in life. Normal events seemed more effortful and I found myself withdrawing from day-to-day activities. I started to feel unsettled for most of the time, waking up early for no apparent reason – often at 4 am – churning thoughts over and over in my mind, and not being able to go back to sleep. I withdrew from people, preferring to be alone. I became snappy and irritable, and felt on edge. My relationships generally suffered, and I lost most of my friendships.

I prefer not to blame all of my problems on my childhood. In fact, my childhood wasn't very eventful relatively speaking, at least not when compared to stories I have heard from many of my clients. I was bullied physically by older children and bullied emotionally by my peers (mainly for being socially backward), and I experienced some mild trauma. Both of my parents were working class people who performed well in their careers and rose through the ranks in their respective emplyment organisations: in my father's case to a top management position. My father was a perfectionist and highly obsessive. His perfectionist nature paid huge dividends for him at work – financially and professionally. He supervised award winning civil engineering work: in fact, I saw an old photograph of him recently, being given an award by the Queen of England. He had a tendency to be obsessive in all areas, including at home, and became angry at even slight violations of his high standards. Let's say as a hormonal teenager, I violated his standards pretty much all of the time and he struggled with parenting me as a teenager. In retrospect, he probably found it difficult to parent me because when he looked at me, he saw himself.

My parents emigrated from Ireland when they were teenagers. They were very young when thrust into the responsibilities of parenthood and as you might expect from young parents, they didn't really have much experience of looking after children, but they were really no different from my friends' parents.

I think my parents did their best to bring me up, based on the knowledge they had, but I struggled with being a child. If I choose to, I can still hear the sound of my mother's voice saying the words she repeated almost daily in her soft Irish accent: 'Childhood are the best years of your life, enjoy it while you can.' This confused me as my childhood felt terrible! And, to make matters worse it seemed like my life was going to go downhill even further if these were the best years of my life. I had low self-esteem, and deeply entrenched beliefs that I was inadequate, stupid, bad, defective, weak, weird, and worthless as a person. I had no one I could talk to, so I kept my fears to myself and spent a lot of my time fighting my beliefs, keeping them hidden while I worked to prove them wrong.

As a young person, there were a number of positives that I could have drawn something from. By the time I reached 15, outsiders would have considered me a privileged child. I had some friends, and I had the support of a well-off family. I lived in a leafy suburb just outside London, and I had gained entry to a state selective grammar school, which at the time was one of the top schools in the country.

Unfortunately, however, I was not able to use what I had been given. By the age of 15, depression had started to hit me quite hard and my motivation to engage in life began to drop significantly. School teachers were not impressed with my academic performance and reported back to my parents that I was underachieving academically. I passed my first set of exams at 16 and went on to do advanced exams, where I achieved less than spectacular results. By the time I was doing my advanced exams, teachers had noticed the changes in my behaviour and had begun to monitor me more closely. One day my chemistry teacher approached me with a frown on his forehead – which seemed to be furrowed even more than usual – muttering, 'If you're not paranoid you should be!' A short time later I was told that the teachers held a meeting about me and I was placed on report: this is where teachers monitor a student much more closely and have regular meetings with them. By then I had dropped out of most of my sports teams such as rugby and cross-country running, I struggled with my friendship groups and eventually found myself dropped from them. Things weren't really going too well from a teenager's point of view. By this time, I already felt that I was a failure in life.

After leaving school you could say that I had a lucky break and gained a position in a small commodity brokers. I struggled to retain this role, not because of my ability to do the technical part of the job, but because of my lack of ability to regulate my mood and deal with interpersonal conflict. Basically, I found it difficult to get on with people. One day I found myself challenging a commodity trader for breaking what I thought were the rules of trading. The problem was that he worked for a very important client. The next day I was invited to my Managing Director's office and given my notice.

A number of further jobs followed, assisted at times by the support of my parents, but again I experienced interpersonal problems and had further dismissals. As time progressed, I found that my CV was beginning to look less and less promising as I moved from one job to another. On paper I thought I had begun to look unemployable and out of desperation began working for financial companies with dubious or unethical outlooks. I soon found that I couldn't work for companies like these, due to my moral stance on life, so I gave up working in the City. Following this, I continued to work my way down the pay scale hierarchy. Eventually the only work I could find was temporary work in factories, delivering pizza, and working as a cleaner for a minimum wage. A friend of mine Joe, a fund manager at Hill Samuel (a leading merchant bank in London at the time) tried to call me and left messages with my parents over a period of several months. I didn't return his calls. I treated him very poorly considering we had developed a close friendship over a number of years. I basically abandoned him with no thought about how it might affect him.

Moving from plush offices to factories and such was a bit of a culture shock for me and I was dismissed from two of my minimum-wage cleaning jobs for not following the requested instructions. I am embarrassed to admit that practically the only job I didn't get the sack from before I was 28 was my pizza delivery job at Pizza Hut, and even that job was painful sometimes. From time-to-time I found myself delivering pizza to some of my-now-successful grammar school peers, who appeared speechless when they opened their door to find me standing there with a pizza for them.

By that time my sense of inadequacy was fully reinforced and I had switched off emotionally. I became quite hard-up financially and my mindset had become quite extreme and rigid. I didn't want to use the unemployment system or to ask my parents for help, as in my mind this would have confirmed to me that I really was not succeeding in life. Sometimes I couldn't earn enough money to pay rent, so I ended up spending months living in a tent at a campsite where the rent was £4 per day. At other times I could pay the rent but was left eating potatoes and baked beans as my only source of nourishment.

I continuously felt that I was failing in some way. I felt empty inside. I just didn't feel like I had the energy to do things; I wanted to escape from my problems and myself. The only time I really felt OK was when I was asleep. I became quite reclusive and more nocturnal. I often did not attend events that I had been invited to, mostly without sending an apology or letting people know. I didn't answer the phone to friends or return their calls. The number of friends I had dwindled to just one. I think the only way that this friend managed to tolerate me was to laugh about the way I behaved, and to recognise that he was not responsible for my behaviour. I felt so insignificant that I genuinely believed other people wouldn't notice or care whether I turned up late for planned events, or would even be bothered if I attended them at all. All my focus was on myself. It was a pitiful kind of self-loathing with endless questioning about why my life was so broken. I was so detached that I had little regard for other people's feelings or my own.

Most of the time I did not want to live anymore and hoped I would die. It was as if my body, mind, and personality were unacceptable to me.

Luckily, in my very late twenties and early thirties I found a few excellent therapists. I worked hard on my therapy - which in my case needed a couple of years, as I had left things for so long before getting help. I brought negative and self-defeating thoughts that I had into conscious awareness and began to make significant changes to my life. I changed my life using many of the processes I have covered in this book. I'm 49 now, and I have been fortunate to have worked with my colleague Dr Nicola Ridgeway in treating several thousand clients over the years, and I haven't looked back since. I am still grateful to have the opportunity to help others who are stuck to free themselves and move on with their lives.

I continue to use many of the exercises and coping strategies that I learnt in my therapy to keep in a good state of well-being. I can state categorically that if I were to stop using my coping strategies now, I would very quickly drift back into mental health problems. I have learnt that psychotherapy is not a quick fix. Many people make initial positive gains after completing a course of therapy, but many relapse after a number of years. An important message I would like to get across, therefore, is that therapy is not a short-term solution to your problems. You will need to keep using what you learn in therapy for the rest of your life: complacency is the biggest risk factor in relapse.

## CHAPTER 1

# Introduction to 'the Black Dog'

The use of the term 'the Black Dog' to describe symptoms of depression can be traced back to 40 BC when it was included in the work of the Roman poet Horace. In more recent times it was made famous by Winston Churchill, the Prime Minister of Great Britain during World War II who often referred to his Black Dog, and the Australian writer and illustrator Matthew Johnstone who wrote the best-selling book, *I had a Black Dog*.

For centuries the Black Dog has been associated with fear, intense pain, and emotional distress. In the literature the Black Dog has a formidable reputation. Run from it, and it will hunt you down relentlessly. Wrestle with it, and it will bare its fangs. Fear it, and it will stalk you unabatedly. Hide from it and it will haunt you until you are all but a shadow of your previous self. Feed it and it will become much bigger than you. For some, suicide feels like the only way to escape from it.

The irony, however, is that the Black Dog is misunderstood. By the time that you finish reading this book you will find out that the Black Dog is not your enemy: nothing could be further from the truth. The Black Dog is loyal and will never let you down. I had my own journey with the Black Dog for many years and at first I didn't have a good relationship with it. I felt that it was ruining my life. This was until I recognised its true intention. The Black Dog has its own language, and follows a specific set of commands and rules. Once you understand the Black Dog, how it operates, and how to communicate with it, you will find that it will happily remain in the background, rather than taking a dominant role in your life.

## What happens when you have the Black Dog?

People who have a visit from the Black Dog are often physically affected by their symptoms for long periods of time: months, or even years. Symptoms can include low mood, reduced or increased appetite, lack of interest in usual activities, poor concentration, increased or reduced sleep, reduced sexual activity, feelings of hopelessness, lack of energy, increased pain perception, thoughts of suicide, feelings of worthlessness, feelings of not being able to function, feeling slowed down, and increased irritation. People may notice these symptoms at different levels, ranging from mild to severe. It is usually the severity and duration of these symptoms that determines whether the Black Dog is classified as mild, moderate, or severe by mental health professionals. Many people with a mild case of the Black Dog can function reasonably well in their day-to-day lives and their depression will often lift by itself without professional help. A severe case of the Black Dog, on the other hand, rarely goes away by itself, can be life threatening, and may cause damage to the brain. As such, it is taken very seriously by health professionals. People who have a visit from the Black Dog will normally have some of the above mentioned symptoms for a period of at least two weeks.* Bear in mind that you do not need to have all of the previously mentioned symptoms to be depressed. In fact, the majority of people who experience the Black Dog can have it without noticing a lack of energy or concentration, and can still achieve pleasure from things. This type of Black Dog can often be very difficult to spot. Even mental health specialists have trouble seeing it. Psychiatrists commonly refer to it as non-melancholic depression.

I have come across non-melancholic depression many times in my clinical work; many people who experience it don't actually realise that they are depressed. It is only when they come out of their depression by taking medication or by having therapy that they begin to really notice how depressed they were.

### Different types of Black Dog

The Diagnostic and Statistical Manual of Mental Disorders V – or DSM-V for short – is a large book that groups together symptoms into various subgroups and categories. Psychiatrists from all over the world meet up to make decisions about the contents of this book and to determine which symptoms grouped together can be classified as a disorder. I have been informed by my esteemed psychiatrist colleagues that these occasions are often intense, heated affairs and that many suggested 'disorders' do not reach the final manuscript, as there needs to be general agreement by psychiatrists, many of whom don't particularly get on with each other. Thus far, the DSM-V has over 40 different ways of classifying the Black Dog, (bi-polar disorder included).

### Reasons for a visit from the Black Dog

If you complete a quick search on Google and look through the main medical websites, you will notice that medical writers find it very difficult to describe any single factor that causes depression. They are very good at describing the many different types of depression that we can suffer from: the DSM-V is evidence of that. They are also very good at identifying risk factors associated with developing adult depression. These include difficulties or trauma in childhood, attention deficit, head injury, genetic factors, personality problems, medical illness, and hormonal changes to name just a few. In reality, however, no one really understands why the Black Dog visits one individual and not another; it appears that the Black Dog is far too complex for that. Perhaps more realistically there are so many types of Black Dog and so many different causal factors that thinking there is just one breed of Black Dog is highly misleading and possibly unhelpful.

*Please note you will not be diagnosed with depression if your low mood is connected to a recent bereavement or a trauma.

# Advice from the Black Dog

I come in many different guises. Many people are unaware that I have been with them until they have had treatment using medication or therapy.

Please take the time to see me. Be curious and interested in me. The suffering that I feel when you refuse to be kind to me adds to the pain that I feel when you scold me or turn your back on me. Don't leave me to despair. Open your heart and welcome me in. I am you and you are me. Together we can live happily.

## CHAPTER 2

# How the brain works

A key to understanding what encouraged the Black Dog to visit is recognising how your brain is organised. There are three main structures that it is important to know about if you experience depression. These areas are the neocortex, the prefrontal cortex, and the subcortical region, (in particular the limbic system and the amygdala, see Figure 1).

## Neocortex

The neocortex is responsible for thinking, planning, and logical thought. We use this part of the brain to understand language, to make calculations, and to problem-solve. The neocortex is used quite a lot when we carry out complex thinking processes.

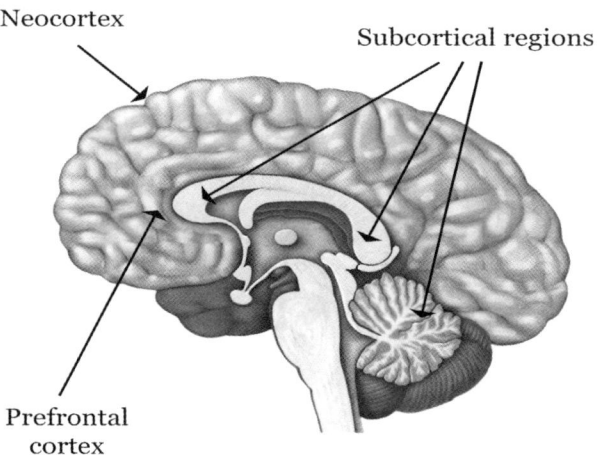

Figure 1. Basic brain organisation

## Prefrontal cortex

The prefrontal cortex is an essential part of the brain for psychological wellness. The prefrontal cortex sits on top of the limbic system, acting as a communication system between the neocortex and the subcortical region. It has many important functions. It quietens down noise in the mind and it can call off or suppress emotional reactions created by subcortical regions. We also use this part of our brain to think about our thinking and to bring choices into conscious awareness. The prefrontal cortex becomes compromised in people with depression and this can often lead to individuals with depression feeling that they are unable to think straight. In more severe cases of depression, the prefrontal cortex stops working properly for long periods, contributing to poor a) concentration, and b) attention.

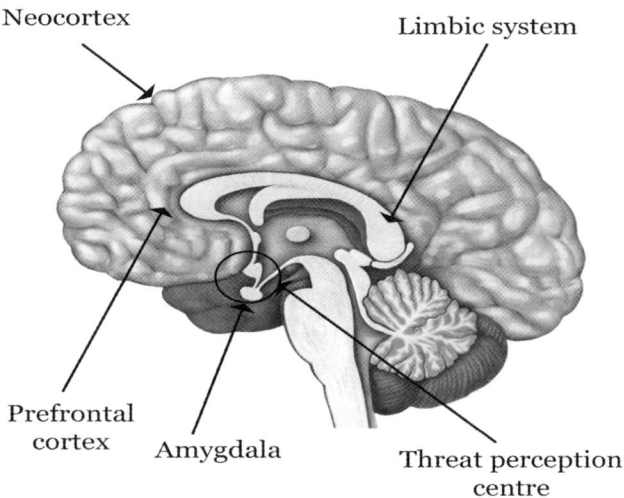

Neocortex

Limbic system

Prefrontal cortex

Amygdala

Threat perception centre

Figure 2.  Structure of the neocortex, prefrontal cortex, and subcortical regions

## The subcortical regions

The subcortical regions, which take their name because they are located underneath the brain's outer cortex area, could be described as a primitive or animal brain, as we share similar brain structures to other mammals.

### The subcortical region and survival

The subcortical regions' (see Figure 2) main interest is survival. The limbic system – a part of the subcortical region – and the areas beneath it, are where emotions are initially triggered. The amygdala (see Figure 2) which is located on both sides of the brain, activates emotions such as anxiety.

Subcortical regions of the brain become highly active when we experience perceived threat; whether real or imagined. When people become highly anxious subcortical brain regions release neurochemicals known as catecholamines which improve the way that primitive brain regions function. In lay terms, catecholamines work a bit like a turbo-boost or a power-up for the animal brain. When primitive brain regions become active, people become more aware of their senses. As a result of this, they may see, hear, feel, taste, and smell things more strongly (Guzman, Tronson, Jovasevic Sato, Guedea, Mizukami, Nishimori & Radulovic, 2013). This process is not without problems, however. Catecholamines, although enhancing the effects of the subcortical region, leach or spread into the nearby prefrontal cortex and stop it functioning effectively. Many people will notice the results of this process as a feeling of mental fuzz or light-headedness. In the majority of cases this leaching effect or mental fuzz is only temporary and when the threat dies down and neurochemicals are reabsorbed, the prefrontal cortex starts to work normally as before.

---

## Examples of how the prefrontal cortex works in real life

The function of the prefrontal cortex won't make much sense unless we examine how it functions in day-to-day existence, so I will draw on some examples from my life. Historically, I have had some difficulties with ice cream. Unfortunately, the ice cream that I like tends to be the expensive type that comes in 500ml tubs with about 1300 calories in. I can't describe the kind of pleasure I get while eating these ice creams from beginning to end, and have tended to use them as a reward over the years, which is not to be advised. After getting into a pattern of eating ice cream for a period of time, I notice that my clothes are starting to feel a bit tight. My neocortex or logical mind comes online and tells me that I am on a path to obesity, possible ill health, difficulties with my pancreas, and heart disease. I look in the mirror and I appear a bit bloated. My partner gently mentions that I may be putting on a little bit of weight, but tells me she still loves me. I don't want to buy a whole new set of clothes. I recognise that I need to stop eating so much ice cream. Luckily, to assist me with my sense of internal conflict, I engage my prefrontal cortex much more to try to correct my habit and bring it into awareness – so that I can make more conscious choices. For example, if I am in the supermarket and I hear a suggestion about ice cream in my mind, I listen to it and then direct my attention to something else instead; perhaps a really interesting book that I am going to read later, or a healthy snack, and I use these things as a replacement reward.

Equally, if I meet a physically attractive person my subcortical region becomes highly stimulated – I recognise that I am an animal after all. My neocortex has a very different idea about a way ahead compared to my subcortical region; I have a great family and things are pretty good in my family life. I am faced with a slight conflict. Luckily, my prefrontal cortex comes online to assist me with my choices. If I am faced with a slight boundary issue or anything that might take me over a fine line in a relationship, I bring it to my awareness, make choices, and put new boundaries around the relationship to limit my fantasy or urge developing any further. My prefrontal cortex helps to suppress the impulses that

I feel, (which often pass within a matter of seconds), and I am able to sustain my happy family existence.

---

## What happens when we experience prolonged threat?

If we experience threat for prolonged periods the continuous release of catecholamines by subcortical regions can gradually damage – or cause atrophy to – the prefrontal cortex located right next to it, (Arnsten, Raskind, Taylor & Connor, 2015). (This generally results in the prefrontal cortex operating much less effectively.) When the prefrontal cortex goes offline or begins to work less effectively we lose our ability to calm ourselves, and we can start to feel more agitated about things that we weren't really bothered about before. This occurs as the prefrontal cortex can no longer suppress emotional reactions triggered by subcortical regions. The neocortex (thinking and analytical brain) is also unable to function effectively as it relies heavily on the prefrontal cortex to make decisions and direct attentional resources. When this occurs some people may notice the emergence of the Black Dog. I have placed a link to a video below which shows how this process works.

**http://www.z1b6.com/4.html**

# Advice from the Black Dog

I will often visit if you have experienced long periods of stress. Unrelenting stress gradually wears down your prefrontal cortex. When this happens it is more difficult to quieten down noise in your mind and to suppress emotional reactions.

Although difficult, this is when I really need your patience and understanding. I need lots of stroking and cuddles, small walks, light meals and a regular sleeping pattern. Only what is nourishing me needs to be considered right now.

## Chapter 3

# What encourages the Black Dog to stay?

Depression is self-perpetuating. By self-perpetuating, I mean that once an individual has a visit from the Black dog, fighting it or hiding from it can fuel further depression. In this respect, once the Black Dog is around it can stay for months, years, or decades.

## How does depression self-perpetuate?

Ignoring the Black Dog for too long can have a significant harmful impact on an individual's functioning through a combination of neurological, biological, cognitive, and behavioural factors. These factors essentially keep symptoms in place. People with depression can experience greater difficulties maintaining healthy relationships with others. The ability to attend and concentrate is affected, which can lead to mistakes at work, or slow down work speed. People with depression find it difficult to remain physically healthy and their motivation reduces. This can lead to self-neglect, which can have further negative health consequences down the line. When people experience depression, information can be viewed in an unbalanced way, which can lead to rash or poor decision-making that can have long-term negative implications. If you think about depression in this way, it is perhaps easy to imagine how somebody who struggles with their relationships, makes poor decisions, underperforms at work, and views the world in a negative way will have a prolonged visit from the Black Dog!

## What do brain scans pick up in depression?

In 2008, the Archives of General Psychiatry, which is a prestigious international journal, published a very interesting study by Thomas Frodl and his colleagues. For three years Thomas Frodl's research team followed 38 individuals with major depressive disorder and compared them to matched non-depressed individuals. During this time, all the study's participants had their brains scanned on a regular basis using a process called high-resolution magnetic resonance imagery. Thomas Frodl and his colleagues found that the individuals with depression experienced a decline in their brain's grey matter, or in other words brain loss or brain atrophy, in specific areas. These areas included the anterior cingulate cortex, an area devoted to conflict resolution, the hippocampus, a very small area of the brain used in memory processing, and the prefrontal cortex. The impact on the prefrontal cortex is especially important to note, because, as I explained earlier, the prefrontal cortex dampens emotions, pushes down irrelevant or interfering stimuli, and helps us to think about our thinking. Although these ideas have been known about by psychologists for over fifty years (Brutkowski, 1965), it is only recently that we are fully beginning to understand how important the prefrontal cortex is for psychological wellness.

Thomas Frodl's study highlights the important neurological implications that prefrontal cortex atrophy has on depression. In essence, a weakened prefrontal cortex could easily explain why individuals with the Black Dog find it so difficult to detach from rumination, which is a process of churning negative thoughts over and over in the mind. With depression there is a compulsion to ruminate, even though many individuals with depression recognise that rumination feeds the Black Dog and keeps it in place.

## Using mindfulness to break patterns of rumination

Personally, I work with clients who have the Black Dog using mindfulness exercises to help them detach from ruminating. Mindfulness exercises involve staying in the present moment, bringing conscious awareness back to the present, and deliberately moving away from thoughts about the past or the future. Even when my clients have learned how to use mindfulness successfully, it can still be very difficult for them to stop ruminating. I will not repeat here what has already been written on mindfulness because there are a number of good books available in this area. Professor Mark Williams has written an excellent book on mindfulness called *Mindfulness: Finding peace in a frantic world* which comes with a CD. If you have the Black Dog I recommend you read his book.

# Advice from the Black Dog

When I visit I will simply wait until you notice me. Please don't try to fight me. If you wrestle with me, you may wear yourself out, and that is the last thing I want. I will also stay longer if you question why I am here.

I can't move without your help. I need you to guide my way. When you shine a light on me, we two can walk free.

## CHAPTER 4

# Serotonin and 5HT

As a chemical messenger, serotonin plays a huge role in the body's overall physical and mental functioning, and this book wouldn't be complete if I didn't mention it. Although most people with the Black Dog may have heard that serotonin is located in the brain, less well known is the fact that most of our serotonin is actually found in our body's digestive system and blood platelets. Only 10 percent of our total serotonin is located in the brain. Brain serotonin can only be produced in the brain. Serotonin is a very important neurotransmitter (chemical messenger) connected to mood, sleep, appetite, memory, sexual function, and social behaviour. Brain serotonin allows brain cells to communicate effectively with one another: usually brain cells throw out serotonin to talk to each other (see Figure 3). Once serotonin has been released it begins to make its way to other cells. While some of the serotonin makes a complete journey to other cells, much of it doesn't, and what's left behind is sucked back in by nearby brain cells for later reuse.

## How anti-depressants work

Many anti-depressant medications come in the form of selective serotonin reuptake inhibitors – SSRIs for short. They work by blocking the serotonin re-uptake process, or more specifically, by reducing the sensitivity of 5HT serotonin receptor sites, or lessening their ability to suck serotonin back in after they have released it (see Figure 4). When SSRIs work well, they effectively leave more serotonin floating about in the area between brain cells. SSRIs do not increase the amount of serotonin the brain produces; they simply help serotonin produced by the brain to become more available. An analogy is to think of a coach with a large squad of basketball players. The coach is using just one or two players in a match against a full team. The players on the court feel defeated and overrun, and the rest of the squad members are just looking on. SSRIs are a bit like the coach bringing on the reserves to help out.

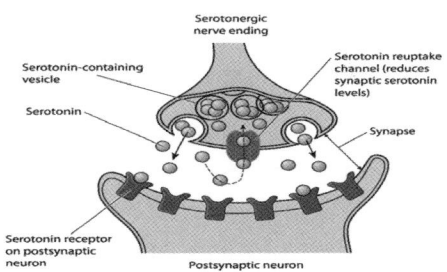

Figure 3. Serotonin communication between cells

## What happens when supplies of serotonin run low?

When supplies of serotonin run low our brain cells begin to lose their ability to communicate with each other, or they 'lose their voice'. One factor that can lead to a Black Dog visit is high cortisol levels. Higher cortisol levels, possibly brought about by a stressful life, tends to result in lower serotonin levels (Dinan, 1994).

## Diet and depression

Researchers suggest that symptoms of the Black Dog may be reduced by feeding stress vulnerable individuals a diet enriched with nutrients essential for the creation of tryptophan before they engage in stressful events, (Markus et al, 2002). Apparently, sea lion has the highest concentrates of tryptophan. Unfortunately, sea lion is not available in most supermarkets, but other foods such as egg-white, spinach, soy protein, seeds, and seaweed also contain relatively high levels of tryptophan compared to other foods. It is difficult to see how this knowledge can be applied in practice, however, as most of us do not recognise that we are more vulnerable to stress and we have no way of measuring how

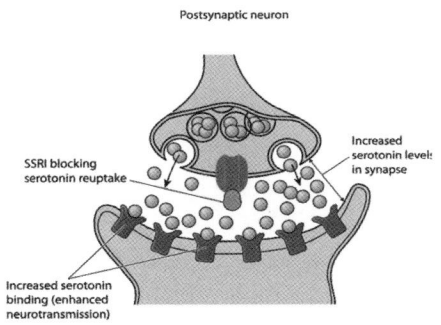

Figure 4. SSRIs increase available serotonin in the brain

much brain serotonin we are using when we are dealing with difficulties. But, I guess a spinach, soya and seaweed omelette wouldn't do any harm.

## How do factors combine to create depression?

Neurological and neurochemical changes dramatically affect the way that we process information. We literally process information differently when we have the Black Dog. Reduced serotonin levels lead to slowed mental functioning. Thinking becomes effortful, and problem-solving ability is not as good as it was before. Additionally, reduced input of the neocortex can lead to the loss of reasoned, balanced thinking which in turn creates an interpretative bias in the way that information is processed. An interpretative bias means that we filter information, so that we only see what our particular filter allows us to see, and not what is really happening. I will cover this area in more detail later on, as an understanding of interpretative bias is fundamental to easing symptoms of depression.

When the prefrontal cortex becomes less active, it has reduced ability to quieten down the chatter of the mind, which leads to increased likelihood of rumination. This means that more valuable neuro-transmitters are used during a mental process that generally achieves no positive results. Reduced input of the prefrontal cortex also means that there is less ability to be self-reflective. In addition, one's attention, concentration, and memory will be negatively affected as the brain tries to process huge amounts of information associated with rumination at the same time. Problem-solving ability slows down and feels more effortful compared with being free from the Black Dog.

If you consider that all the above is happening at the same time, it is not surprising that so many of us can find ourselves stuck in a negative cycle. I have placed a picture of this cycle on the next page (see Figure 5). The basic neurochemical and biological features of the Black Dog reduce our ability to function, making it more difficult to climb out of it.

As I found personally for more than ten years, people can get really stuck when they have the Black Dog. With a more negative or skewed view of the world, people are more likely to want to avoid us. When we have depression we can lose friends or acquaintances, on top of our other problems.

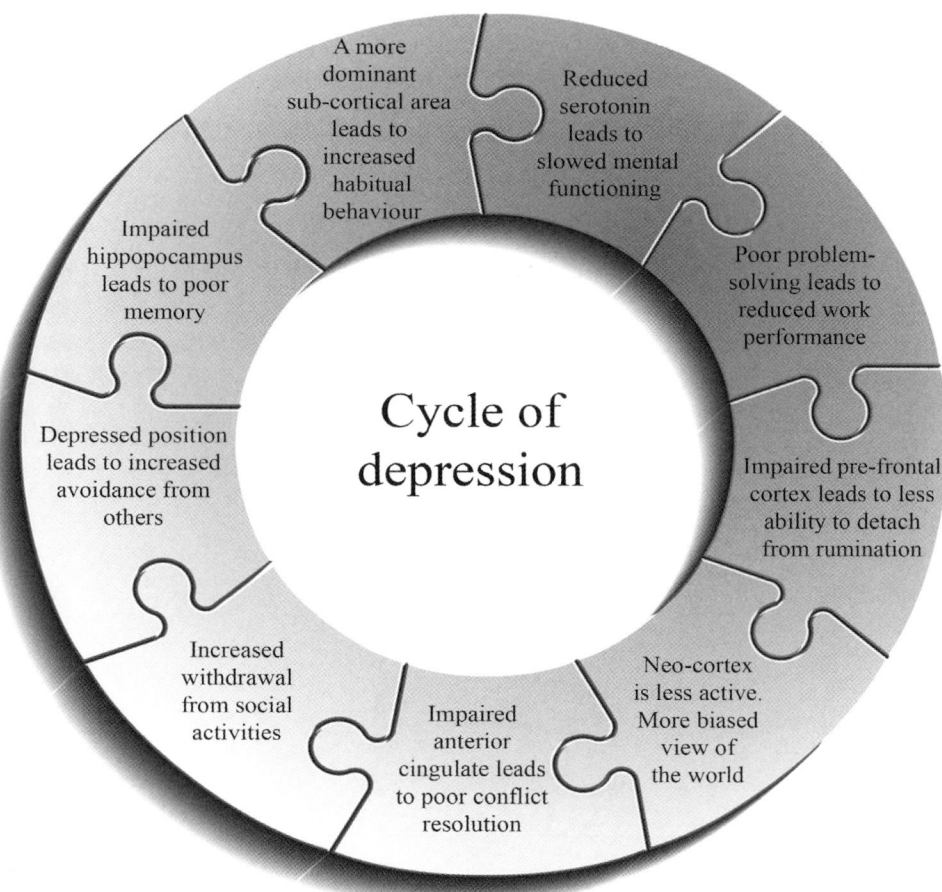

Figure 5. Cycle of depression

# Advice from the Black Dog

I will visit you when your serotonin levels run low. Stress and high cortisol levels reduce levels of brain serotonin. When this happens I will slow you down to protect you. At this point do you best to surrender and let go. Your tears of frustration can then quickly shift to tears of relief. Rest and kindness with baby steps at this point will be essential and helpful.

## CHAPTER 5

# Getting to know your Black Dog

Most of the time memory alone is unreliable when it comes to recalling what activities impact on mood. Often the most valid way to assess your mood is to make a record while you are experiencing it. Keeping track of your mood will help you to identify external or internal aspects of your life that are concerning your Black Dog. When I say external aspects, I mean the things that happen around you, or specific events that you can observe through your senses. Internal aspects are what happen in your mind, or more specifically, your thoughts, feelings, and bodily reactions.

## Mood diaries

I have placed a weekly mood diary on the following page for you to complete. Use this diary to make a simple record of your mood over the course of a week.

You can also use my online questionnaire to keep track of your symptoms, and to assess how your symptoms improve over time by following this link.

**http://www.z1b6.com/7.html**

## Activity schedule

An activity schedule is a very powerful tool to assist you with your mood. In most cases, measures of enjoyment and achievement are recorded, although you can also pick other categories, that are more relevant to you. As a tool the activity schedule encourages you to think about activities that improve your mood and enhance your life.

The general idea is to record measures of your achievement and enjoyment on an hourly basis, and to do this over a period of a week. An activity schedule will help you to become much more aware of life events and lifestyle factors that contribute to your mood state. You can find different versions of these forms on the following pages.

Table 1. Mood dairy

**Day** _____  **Date** _____

| Time period | Positive feeling 0 to 10 | Negative feeling 0 to 10 |
|---|---|---|
| 6am to 12pm | | |
| 12pm to 6pm | | |
| 6pm to 12am | | |

**Day** _____  **Date** _____

| Time period | Positive feeling 0 to 10 | Negative feeling 0 to 10 |
|---|---|---|
| 6am to 12pm | | |
| 12pm to 6pm | | |
| 6pm to 12am | | |

**Day** _____  **Date** _____

| Time period | Positive feeling 0 to 10 | Negative feeling 0 to 10 |
|---|---|---|
| 6am to 12pm | | |
| 12pm to 6pm | | |
| 6pm to 12am | | |

**Day** _____  **Date** _____

| Time period | Positive feeling 0 to 10 | Negative feeling 0 to 10 |
|---|---|---|
| 6am to 12pm | | |
| 12pm to 6pm | | |
| 6pm to 12am | | |

**Day** _____  **Date** _____

| Time period | Positive feeling 0 to 10 | Negative feeling 0 to 10 |
|---|---|---|
| 6am to 12pm | | |
| 12pm to 6pm | | |
| 6pm to 12am | | |

**Day** _____  **Date** _____

| Time period | Positive feeling 0 to 10 | Negative feeling 0 to 10 |
|---|---|---|
| 6am to 12pm | | |
| 12pm to 6pm | | |
| 6pm to 12am | | |

**Day** _____  **Date** _____

| Time period | Positive feeling 0 to 10 | Negative feeling 0 to 10 |
|---|---|---|
| 6am to 12pm | | |
| 12pm to 6pm | | |
| 6pm to 12am | | |

**Day** _____  **Date** _____

| Time period | Positive feeling 0 to 10 | Negative feeling 0 to 10 |
|---|---|---|
| 6am to 12pm | | |
| 12pm to 6pm | | |
| 6pm to 12am | | |

**Day** _____  **Date** _____

| Time period | Positive feeling 0 to 10 | Negative feeling 0 to 10 |
|---|---|---|
| 6am to 12pm | | |
| 12pm to 6pm | | |
| 6pm to 12am | | |

## Mood Diary

Please use this diary to keep a record of your mood. For each time period give yourself a score between 0 and 10 where 10 is the most that you can experience a feeling.

For the positive feeling box please rate how positive you felt during each time period as a whole. Examples of positivity may include being interested, excited, enthusiastic, strong, proud etc.

For the negative feeling box please rate how negative you felt during the time period. Examples of negativity may include feeling distressed, hostile, afraid, upset, ashamed and such like.

Table 2. Mood dairy (days)

| Activity schedule | | Monday | | | Tuesday | | | Wednesday | | | Thursday | | | Friday | | | Saturday | | | Sunday | | |
|---|---|---|---|---|---|---|---|---|---|---|---|---|---|---|---|---|---|---|---|---|---|---|
| Time | | Activity | H | A | Activity | H | A | Activity | H | A | Activity | H | A | Activity | H | A | Activity | H | A | Activity | H | A |
| 8am to 9am | Write down the main thing that you are doing in each hour period. | | | | | | | | | | | | | | | | | | | | | |
| 9am to 10am | | | | | | | | | | | | | | | | | | | | | | |
| 10am to 11am | After you have completed the activity score yourself in terms of achievement and happiness giving yourself a score | | | | | | | | | | | | | | | | | | | | | |
| 11am to 12pm | | | | | | | | | | | | | | | | | | | | | | |
| 12m to 1pm | | | | | | | | | | | | | | | | | | | | | | |
| 1pm to 2pm | between 0 and 10, where 10 is the highest it can possibly be and 0 is the lowest. | | | | | | | | | | | | | | | | | | | | | |
| 2pm to 3pm | | | | | | | | | | | | | | | | | | | | | | |
| 3pm to 4pm | H- Happiness A-Achievement | | | | | | | | | | | | | | | | | | | | | |
| 4pm to 5pm | | | | | | | | | | | | | | | | | | | | | | |
| 5pm to 6pm | | | | | | | | | | | | | | | | | | | | | | |
| 6pm to 7pm | | | | | | | | | | | | | | | | | | | | | | |
| 7pm to 8pm | | | | | | | | | | | | | | | | | | | | | | |
| 8pm to 9pm | | | | | | | | | | | | | | | | | | | | | | |

Table 3. Mood dairy (no days)

**Activity schedule**

| Time | Activity | | Activity | | Activity | | Activity | | Activity | | Activity | | Activity | |
|---|---|---|---|---|---|---|---|---|---|---|---|---|---|---|
| | H | A | H | A | H | A | H | A | H | A | H | A | H | A |
| | | | | | | | | | | | | | | |
| | | | | | | | | | | | | | | |
| | | | | | | | | | | | | | | |
| | | | | | | | | | | | | | | |
| | | | | | | | | | | | | | | |
| | | | | | | | | | | | | | | |
| | | | | | | | | | | | | | | |
| | | | | | | | | | | | | | | |
| | | | | | | | | | | | | | | |
| | | | | | | | | | | | | | | |
| | | | | | | | | | | | | | | |

Write down the main thing that you are doing in each hour time period.

After you have completed the activity score yourself in terms of achievement and happiness giving yourself a score between 0 and 10, where 10 is the highest it can possibly be and 0 is the lowest.

H- Happiness
A- Achievement

Table 4. Mood dairy (blank)

**Activity schedule**

Write down the main thing that you are doing in each hour time period.

| Time | Activity | Activity | Activity | Activity | Activity | Activity | Activity |
|------|----------|----------|----------|----------|----------|----------|----------|
|  |  |  |  |  |  |  |  |
|  |  |  |  |  |  |  |  |
|  |  |  |  |  |  |  |  |
|  |  |  |  |  |  |  |  |
|  |  |  |  |  |  |  |  |
|  |  |  |  |  |  |  |  |
|  |  |  |  |  |  |  |  |
|  |  |  |  |  |  |  |  |
|  |  |  |  |  |  |  |  |
|  |  |  |  |  |  |  |  |
|  |  |  |  |  |  |  |  |
|  |  |  |  |  |  |  |  |

Table 5. Daily diary

## Daily activity diary

| Time | Activity | Enjoyment 0 to 10 | Attainment 0 to 10 |
|------|----------|-------------------|--------------------|
|      |          |                   |                    |

Table 5. Daily diary

# Advice from the Black Dog

Keeping track of your mood will help you to draw attention to aspects of your life that may be keeping your low mood in place.

It really is a great opportunity to stop and reflect on your day-to-day life and to consider yourself a truly worthy subject.

Taking a noticing perspective is the beginning of non-judgemental awareness of yourself. This will ultimately lead to the development of a much more authentic and compassionate relationship with yourself.

## CHAPTER 6

# Consider going to a Black Dog expert!

I struggled with the Black Dog for more than a decade before I recognised that all along it really was my best friend. To be honest, I thought I was incurable and nobody could help me. I was pretty nervous before I went along to my first therapy session. On the recommendation of a friend I drove to see a lovely, kind, and exceptionally skilful lady in Cambridge, England called Jenny. She worked from a room in her house, which I guess her family would have used as their conservatory when she wasn't working with her clients.

In my first number of sessions I got caught up in what Jenny might think of me. As a client, I was anything but open. I was very careful about what I said, and held back a good 95 percent of my darkest fears and insecurities, wanting to hide my real sense of inadequacy. When I think back, I guess this is not surprising. Talking about my problems felt very unfamiliar to me, and deep down inside I believed that I was intrinsically bad. Also, I wanted Jenny to like me! I thought she wouldn't like me or want to work with me if she knew what I was really like. While all this was going on I was being harassed by a stream of thoughts running through my mind, which went something along the lines of 'Jenny doesn't really care about you!', 'You're paying her to be nice to you!', and 'She's only nice because she's doing her job and who knows what she really thinks about you!' (Incidentally, I met Jenny several years later in professional environments and found out that she really was a lovely person, even when she wasn't being paid.)

In our sessions, I became strongly aware that Jenny provided a lot of structure and containment. I sensed a subtle and gentle influence guiding me towards the present rather than drifting back into the past. When Jenny asked me what I wanted to work on I really didn't know. I started off by saying 'I don't know' but, as you might recognise, that really didn't give my therapy a great deal of focus. Fortunately, Jenny helped me to focus on some specific problems. I soon discovered that self-disclosure worked like an old engine that had been left idle for years. After a stuttering start, I gradually became accustomed to opening up and I eventually got into a flow. I felt that Jenny understood what was happening to me. She drew out many things that I said using diagrams on a sheet of paper and even by the end of my first appointment I certainly felt I understood a lot more about myself.

# Preparing yourself for therapy

If you want to give yourself some focus before you start your therapy, it will be worth making a list of problems that you are experiencing at the earliest stage possible. Often it may not be possible to work with every problem you have on your list. However, a list will provide you with an opportunity to help you prioritise your concerns, and highlight which problems distress you the most.

If you have limited funding for your therapy or the number of sessions you have been offered is fixed, focusing on one specific area or working on just one problem at a time will help you to manage your expectations. A problem list is something that you can come back to at regular intervals to assess progress.

---

**An example of a problem list**

1.  I find it difficult to be assertive in my relationships.
2.  I don't have many friends.
3.  I constantly worry about losing my job.
4.  I am impulsive with money.
5.  I become concerned if I find people don't like me.
6.  I feel agitated a lot of the time.

---

**Therapy preparation sheet**

Once you have a problem list, you can use a therapy preparation sheet to help narrow your focus further still.

Generally, establishing a desired outcome early on in therapy aids ongoing review processes, and enhances motivation. In basic terms, filling in a therapy preparation sheet will help you to recognise what you are aiming for.

Table 6. Therapy preparation sheet

## Therapy preparation sheet

**Describe the problem that I have been experiencing**

I keep arguing with my partner in front of my children. The arguments are often over pointless little things and they make my children anxious and upset.

**How long has this problem been around for?**

This problem has been around for as long as I can remember. We both have a problem backing down.

**What may have triggered this problem?**

Being told that I have done something wrong is the main trigger, or being criticised.

**How have I attempted to resolve my problem?**

I try to keep the conversation short if I see an argument beginning, but my partner then starts to become anxious that I am being distant.

**What are the main things that keep my problem in place?**

Arguing back generally makes it worse. If I criticise my partner back it can end up in a war that seems to go on for days.

**What will I need to do to resolve this problem?**

Find a different way to reacting to my partner's comments. It takes two people to keep the argument going.

**How would my life be different without this problem?**

Life would be more peaceful and there would be less negative energy floating around the house. The children would feel more relaxed.

## Therapy preparation sheet

**Describe the problem that I have been experiencing**

**How long has this problem been around for?**

**What may have triggered this problem?**

**How have I attempted to resolve my problem?**

**What are the main things that keep my problem in place?**

**What will I need to do to resolve this problem?**

**How would my life be different without this problem?**

# Advice from the Black Dog

Dealing with the problems that you have in your life or approaching your difficulties in a different way can result in a significant improvement in your mood.

We are naturally driven to avoid anything painful, whether that is physical or emotional pain. If there are problems in out lives, especially those that keep rearing their heads, we must stop and examine them.

Often the very first step of acknowledging that a problem exists can be very relieving in itself.

## CHAPTER 7

# Making a start using CBT

At his point it will be useful to introduce the concept of cogntive behaviour therapy (CBT). A fundamental principle behind all CBT approaches is the way that we think affects the way that we feel. At its most simplest, CBT involves bringing thinking and behaviour patterns into awareness, evaluating them, and then if necessary changing them.

To make a start using CBT it will be important to identify distressing thoughts, and to notice what changes occur within your body when you have these thoughts.

Basically, subcortical brain regions listen in to all of our thoughts in order to keep our bodies a little bit ahead of us, preparing us physiologically for whatever we might need to do next. If we think about eating a lemon, our mouths will start to salivate slightly. This happens before we get anywhere near a lemon. The best way I can think to explain how the subcortical region works is to compare it to my dog when I take her for a walk. She often pulls

'Hey wait…I said it's getting dark…not park!'

at her lead, chocking herself. She doesn't know where she's going, but it seems like she always wants to be first.

## We need to recognise that the brain works holistically

The brain works holistically. By holistic I mean most parts of the brain work at the same time, or in parallel, and they are directly connected to other parts. Information travels through the brain in microseconds. As a result, the subcortical regions of the brain, where emotions spring from, have access to every thought that occurs within the mind very quickly. If you think about it deeply enough you will recognise that not all thoughts generate feelings: the main thoughts that generate feelings are those that are more directly linked to our survival as human beings. These are likely to be thoughts connected to our social conduct, our financial future, reproduction, physical security, friendships, family, food, and social status. Indeed, as it is often suggested, emotions are the basic survival mechanisms that helped our ancestors to survive, resulting in us being alive right now.

## We ruminate more when we are depressed

When we experience depression we ruminate about things that we would not normally be bothered about. In my experience, people ruminate more because the prefrontal cortex is less able to quieten down noise in the mind. Negative and critical thoughts are more likely to reach awareness because the prefrontal cortex is less able to screen them out. People ruminate as they attempt to find solutions to cope with self-critical thoughts that are actually generated by their own ruminative processes. Further rumination tends to produce even more negative thoughts. This activates the subcortical regions' threat responses even more, and reduces the input of the neocortex. This effectively means that people think less rationally when they have depression and they can get stuck in a ruminative loop/cycle.

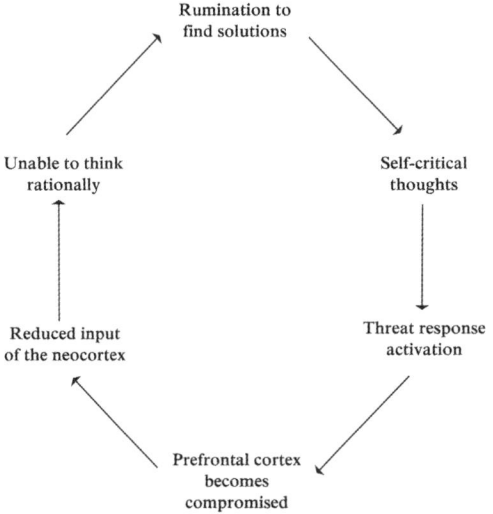

'Rumination can be self-perpetuating'

# Advice from the Black Dog

Rumination can be draining and uses up a lot of mental resources. What's odd is that we genuinely believe that ruminating (or asking 'why' questions), to work out why we feel low will actually help. Nothing could be further from the truth. Churning ideas over can be very helpful as a problem-solving strategy but it doesn't work as a way of getting rid of low mood. Unfortunately, through no fault of your own, rumination will make you feel a lot worse.

## CHAPTER 8

# Avoidance and safety behaviours

The use of avoidance is a common habit for people who experience depression. Avoidance involves deliberately staying away from situations that might create emotional distress. Many people find it stressful to be around others when they have depression. This might be because they think others will judge them negatively, or they feel that they have to try to put on a performance and pretend to be how they normally are. People are more likely to use safety behaviours to reduce their distress when they approach situations that they fear. Both avoidance and safety behaviours tend to keep people's problems in place, and as time progresses continued use of them can lead to a gradual loss of self-confidence resulting in further mood deterioration.

## How overuse of avoidance causes problems

There is a major problem with using safety behaviours and avoidance when the Black Dog is around. The more we use safety behaviours and avoidance, the more automatic these strategies become. It is natural for us to experience a sense of relief when we carry out a behaviour that removes pain or reduces distress. In psychological terms this process is referred to as negative reinforcement. Negative reinforcement occurs when we carry out certain behaviours to remove painful feelings. Over time, as processes are repeated and memory pathways are laid down, we begin to automatically engage in these behaviours without thinking, (see Figures 6 & 7).

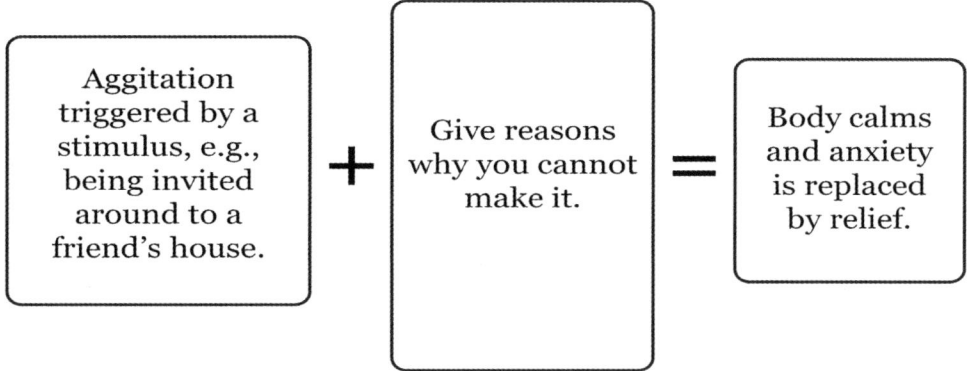

Figure 6: Negative reinforcement

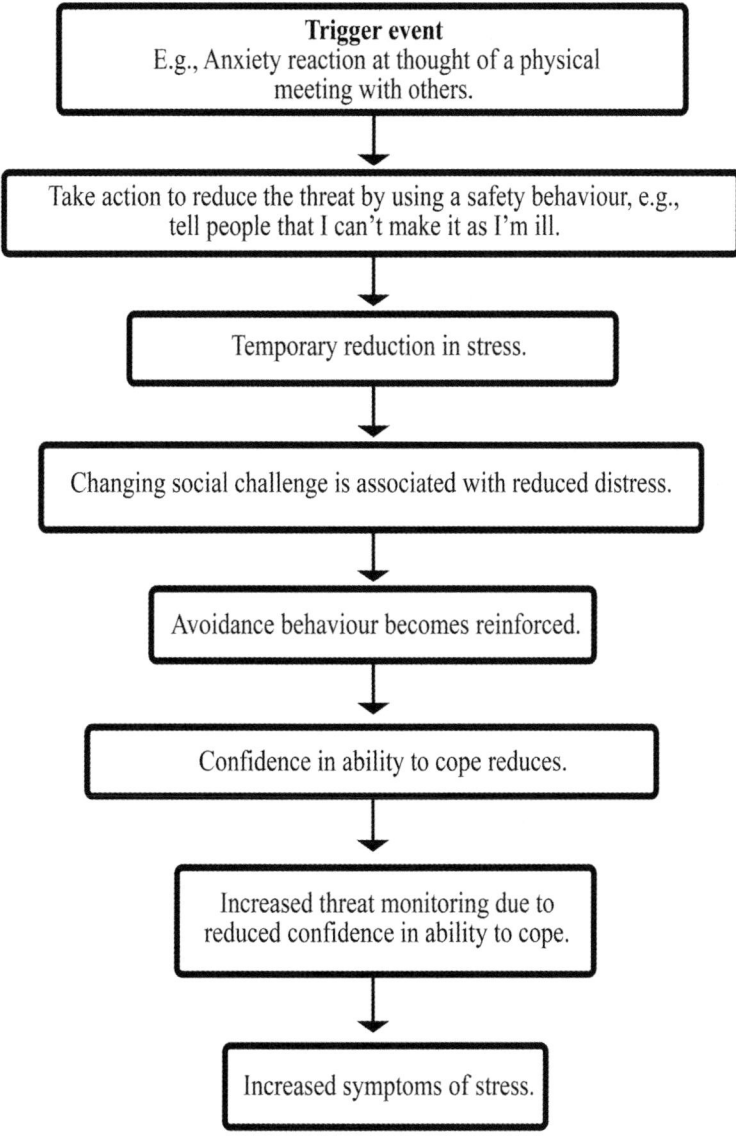

Figure 7: Example of negative reinforcement in action

# Advice from the Black Dog

If you feel ashamed of me and avoid activities that you used to enjoy I am likely to feel even more unsettled and bother you more. Take me with you to the things you used to enjoy. Winston Churchill kept me on his lap while he made important decisions on behalf of Great Britain during World War II.

I need to know that I'm not a burden to you and that my presence won't stop you doing things. If you take my lead lightly, pat me and soothe me as you go, I can walk along quite easily beside you.

## CHAPTER 9

# Self-observation

To understand what made the Black Dog pay you a visit you will need to begin observing yourself. The first thing that I will invite you to notice is that you are having thoughts and feelings. The second thing that I would like you to recognise is that you have a range of thoughts, feelings, and behaviours under different circumstances. Once you become aware that your thoughts and feelings fluctuate, you can monitor how you react in different situations. One of the best and most accurate ways to complete self-observation is by writing things down using diaries.

Ideally you will approach your thoughts with an intention of becoming really curious about what you will notice. Try to develop an interest in the different types of thoughts that you experience and the feelings or sensations that accompany your thoughts. Carrying out self-observation is not designed to encourage you to judge yourself: bear in mind that noticing a critical or self-judgemental thought is very different to listening to or believing that thought.

When I first had therapy, I had an aversion to writing and filling in charts. Writing things down didn't really appeal to me, but I didn't discount the idea that it might work much better for others. Eventually, my therapist Jenny convinced me to fill in the sheets and I found that they actually helped with my mood. I noticed I could stand back from myself more. I started to realise I had many more feelings than I previously thought. I saw that a lot of the things I was doing in my personal life I didn't actually enjoy. I started to see that there were things missing from my life. I wasn't consciously aware of these things before I started observing myself. Once I realised there was an animal part to the mind, I began to notice when it came online much more and how it affected the way that I thought. I recognised that my analytical mind and my feeling mind didn't always agree. I started listening to both parts of my mind and then made decisions after thinking about my life in a more balanced way.

It wasn't obvious to me before I began observing myself that for every thought, feeling, or behaviour I noticed, I had a choice about how to react or respond. Before this, I was just living a bit like a puppet, acting automatically. It also helped me not to judge my thoughts and feelings. I felt so much more confident once I noticed I didn't need to react to every thought or feeling that I had.

## Self-observation as a scientific approach

A fundamental aspect of any scientific approach is accurate observation. When you are able to stand back mentally and think about your own thinking processes, this will enable you to increase your awareness of your thoughts, feelings, and behaviours, particularly when you have the Black Dog. This process of self-observation will assist you to become aware of the cycles that you engage in when you become emotionally distressed.

There are many different types of diaries that can be used to help you with your Black Dog, but most involve recording combinations of thoughts, physiological reactions, feelings/emotions, and behaviours. Diaries encourage the use of regular body scanning, which will be beneficial to you as body scanning a) creates greater sensory awareness and b) encourages increased experiential learning. Experiential learning occurs when people learn through their senses and feelings rather than through thinking or reading.

Specific body changes that you may notice when you are upset could be increased tension, emptiness, tight chest, pounding head, heart racing, heavy feelings in the legs, and such like. Many physiological reactions connected to emotions are very similar: for example, the physiological changes associated with anxiety and anger. But, bodily reactions can be perceived very differently, and trigger different consequential behaviours. This is why it is important to label the emotion that accompanies your physiological reaction.

If you would like to look at an example of a thought, feeling, and behaviour sheet that people fill in, I have placed an example overleaf (see Table 7). A further example (see Table 8) and blank sheets for you to use are also available (see Tables 9 and 10). Most commonly, people complete thought, feelings, and behaviour sheets for situations that they think they have not handled as well as they could have.

### Can self-observation increase the effectiveness of the prefrontal cortex?

The brain is well known by neurologists – who are medical experts in the brain – to have high levels of plasticity. Plasticity means that the brain has the ability to repair itself and grow in size the more that it is used. Neuropsychologist, Professor Eleanor Maguire from Ireland has published over 100 research articles and book chapters on the neuropsychology of the brain. The majority of her research has focused on memory, the hippocampus (an important brain area connected to memory) and the subcortical brain regions surrounding it. In perhaps one of her most famous papers dating back to the 1990s, she and her colleagues reported the results of their investigation into the brains of London taxi drivers. London taxi drivers were a very useful 'real life' experiment at the time, as there was a requirement that all taxi drivers complete a process known as 'the knowledge'. This required London taxi drivers to spend a large amount of time memorising the spatial layout of London streets – or exercising their hippocampi. If they did not pass 'the knowledge' test they could not become a taxi driver in London. Eleanor Maguire used a process known as structural magnetic resonance imagery – a type of brain scan – to measure the hippocampal sizes of participating taxi drivers. She found that London taxi drivers had significantly larger hippocampi than matched non-taxi drivers of a similar level of intelligence, and the more experience a taxi driver had, the larger their hippocampus was. Eleanor Maguire's results show us that there is the potential to grow and strengthen any brain area through cognitive exercise, and this includes the prefrontal cortex.

## Advice on using thought diaries

A key area for you to become aware of when completing diaries is to notice the thoughts that you have in your mind. Become curious about your thoughts and approach them as an interested observer. Thoughts do not need to mean anything about you and thoughts cannot make you do anything that you don't want to do.

NB. If you find that using thought diaries acts as a trigger for you to ruminate then you are best off discontinuing using thought diaries at this stage. You can return to them later on when you have learned how to complete decoupling cognitive exercises – covered later on in this book. You may also not be able to complete thought records at times when you are feeling really upset. If you feel that you can't complete a thought record when you are feeling down, simply take out a thought record later (when you feel less distressed) and remind yourself about what happened.

## Thought, feeling/physiology and behaviour diaries

Generally, most of us live our lives automatically, without giving much thought to: a) thinking about our thinking, b) how we react to our feelings or c) what makes us behave the way that we do. Completing a diary brings more of these automatic processes into our awareness. Once these patterns are brought into our conscious awareness, we immediately have more choice about how to react. This is due to the fact that writing information down about the self encourages a process of stepping back and observing.

Table 7. Example of Situation, thought, feeling, and behaviour sheet

**Thoughts, feelings & behaviour diary**

| Time:<br>Date:<br>Trigger situation | Thoughts, e.g., 'They must think that I'm an idiot' | Emotion, e.g., anxiety, anger, shame, disgust | Behaviour, e.g., avoid situation |
|---|---|---|---|
| 16.00pm<br>9 July<br>Not being invited to a colleague's wedding | 'She practically invited everyone else in the office apart from me. When she's got no one else to talk to she wants to be my friend.' | Feel low and angry. I feel irritated being around her. | Ignore her whenever possible.<br><br>Others start to think I am behaving oddly and ask me what's wrong. I just say everything's fine. |

Table 8:  A further example of a thought, feeling and behaviour diary

**Thoughts, feelings & behaviour diary**

| Time:<br>Date:<br>Trigger situation | Thoughts, e.g., 'They must think that I'm an idiot' | Emotion, e.g., anxiety, anger, shame, disgust | Behaviour, e.g., avoid situation |
|---|---|---|---|
| 12.00pm<br>6 June<br>Disagreement with an opposing football coach. | 'He's going along with the referee's decision because it's easier for him. My reaction  shows that there is something wrong with me. He's laughing at me and thinks I'm an idiot.' | Anxiety, anger, guilt, shame. | Raise a formal protest. Think of some different ways in which I can get him back. Churn the situation over in my mind for a couple of days. Feel guilty and ashamed about the way that I am thinking. |

## Thoughts, feelings & behaviour diary

| Time:<br>Date:<br>Trigger situation | Thoughts, e.g., 'They must think that I'm an idiot' | Emotion, e.g., anxiety, anger, shame, disgust | Behaviour, e.g., avoid situation |
|---|---|---|---|
| | | | |

## Thought, emotion, physiology, and behaviour sheet

| | |
|---|---|
| **Day:**<br><br>**Time:**<br><br>**Trigger situation:** | **Thoughts:** |

### Physiological reactions

| | |
|---|---|
| **Emotion:** | **Behaviour:** |

# Advice from the Black Dog

Observing your thoughts, feelings and behaviours/actions is the beginning point of moving me away from feeling so dark. Being under attack everyday from streams of negative thoughts and feelings keeps me horribly stuck and unhappy.

Self-observation will help you to bring negative thoughts that are running in the back of your mind to the forefront of your mind. Once you become aware of how your thoughts influence the way that you feel, you will be in a better position to change things.

## CHAPTER 10

# Cognitive distortions

In previous chapters I stated that when we become distressed, the way that we think can change. I also mentioned that the way we think can affect the way that we view the world, the way we feel, and the way we behave. I'd like to progress these ideas a little further now by covering cognitive distortions.

High levels of distress can distort our perception, mood, and behaviour, directly affecting the way we make sense of things. When this occurs our thinking style can move from being balanced, flexible, expansive, and considered to a more rigid style.

Early on in my therapy sessions, I recognised the amount of cognitive distortions I had in my thinking. The best way I can think to explain it is to imagine that someone puts some glasses on you, but you don't realise that you're wearing them. The glasses can make things seem much bigger or smaller than they really are.

When I began work with my therapist she helped me to realise that when I got upset I didn't always see the world clearly. Sometimes I filtered information so that I only saw what my mind would let me see. This meant I had a limited viewpoint and could not see what was really happening!

'I'm so glad that you could all make it today…'

At other times, I felt that I knew what was going to happen before it actually happened.

'Looks like it's going to be terrible
tonight! I think I had better stay in.'

And, everywhere I looked, I could see danger. .

It is vital in your journey with your Black Dog that you learn to recognise when cognitive distortions are occurring so that as time progresses you can learn how to detach from them. I have placed a table of some of the more common thinking distortions for you to have a look at on the next page, (see Table 11).

I also usually have a speech ready to tell my clients. It goes something like this:  The moment we say to ourselves 'Nothing ever works for me. He or she always does that to me or I'm never considered', this will become our reality at that moment in time. If it were true that nothing ever worked out, that all people always behave like this to us, all of the time, and that we were never considered, that indeed would be a pretty despairing place to be. Instead, how about if we choose to have awareness, without judgement of our thinking style? This will allow us to quickly acknowledge obvious distortions. This acknowledgement alone can have a marked positive impact on how we feel. Isn't it so much more refreshing to be able to stand back from seeing the 'alls' and 'everythings' as facts and notice them instead as thinking styles, or momentary beliefs!

Table 11: Thinking biases/cognitive distortions

### Thinking biases and what to look out for

**All or nothing thinking:** Viewing things as either right or wrong; there is no middle ground. Things are either perfect or fundamentally flawed. There is just black or white, grey does not exist, e.g., always/never, good/bad.

**Personalising:** Focusing on things in the immediate environment and connecting it to the self. Thinking for example, 'She did that deliberately because she knew that I wouldn't like that!' The world revolves around the self.

**Mental filtering:** Selecting specific negative ideas to dwell on and ignoring all of the positive ones.

**Disqualifying the positive:** Positives don't count, there is nothing special about the way I did it, e.g., 'That only happened because I was lucky.'

**Distorted images:** Using images as evidence. A picture or image in the mind that reflects extreme themes of fear, sadness, disgust, pain, etc.

**Fortune telling:** Predicting the future in a negative way without any real evidence, e.g., 'It's going to be terrible'; 'It will be a disaster'; 'I just know it.'

**Shoulds, oughts & musts:** Having ideas that things can only be done one way: 'People should ...'; 'I must ...'; 'I really ought to ...'; 'He shouldn't have ...'

**Over-generalising:** Taking single events or circumstances and viewing them as happening more often than they really do. Thinking that things happen everywhere.

**Emotional reasoning:** Using emotions as evidence, e.g., 'I feel it, so it must be true.'

**Mind reading:** Drawing conclusions about what others are thinking without any evidence, e.g.;'She doesn't like me'; 'They think I am stupid.'

# Advice from the Black Dog

Depression can lead you to view your life as much worse than it really is. Feelings can make your thoughts seem more real but it doesn't make them any more accurate.

Certain damaging behaviours are often the result of being influenced by extreme thoughts and feelings. The results of these behaviours can lead to us feeling more depressed with even more distortions in our thinking.

## CHAPTER 11

# Rules

We all live by rules and most of the time our rules help us. They work automatically in the background of our minds helping us to make our way through cultural conventions and social occasions. We have literally hundreds of rules that guide our behaviour: for example, rules about queuing up, the way we drive our car, what to do when we attend a dinner party, how to use a knife and fork, what clothing to wear on what occasion, etc. Most of the time we are completely unaware of our rules unless someone breaks them; for example, if somebody pushes in front of us in a queue, talks out loud in a library, and so on.

Many of us also have rules that we use to protect ourselves from our deepest fears: for example, 'If I do everything right and make no mistakes at all times, then I will be OK'.

During my therapy I discovered that the rules I had were mainly about how I wanted others to perceive me. They were a bit of a surprise to me when I noticed them. I kind of knew they were there in the background but hadn't really thought about them in that way before. My rules were something along the lines of: 'If I produce results and I am contributing at all times, then I will be OK.' And: 'If I meet the highest standards at all times, then I will be OK.' My rules meant that I spent most of my time working and not spending time with my family. If I wasn't working, I felt as though something wasn't quite right. I found it difficult to stop and rest even for five minutes. If I stopped working I felt guilty or anxious. It felt wrong if I wasn't achieving something.

On one occasion, I took on a difficult role at work. I worked and worked until eventually I became exhausted. When I wasn't able to work the way I did before, I felt guilty and started beating myself up over it. My partner told me I was neglecting her, that she was unhappy in our relationship and my children said that I didn't spend any time with them. When I thought about what was happening it really brought what I was doing to my attention. I thought I was doing all the extra work to help my family but obviously it didn't feel that way to them.

## How our rules can leave us feeling stuck

In about 90% of the people who have brought their Black Dog to me, their dog has come to visit as a result of continuous rule violations. A good example of this happened with a client I once worked with called Joan. Joan was an attractive married lady in her early fifties who worked as a personal assistant to a European chief executive officer of a multi-national company. When I spoke to Joan on the phone to arrange her assessment appointment she told me that she could only come for an assessment in the evening after work. She hinted that an appointment with me was inconvenient for her and she was only meeting me because her psychiatrist had asked her to. Early in our meeting I began to recognise how tired I felt and wondered how I would manage to remain awake until the end of our session. After a while, I recognised that this feeling wasn't coming from me; it was coming from Joan. Joan told me that she had been feeling fatigued for about two months and over the past few weeks she had begun to work longer hours and was beginning to feel exhausted by it. I asked her what had led to her increased work hours. She told me that this was because she didn't feel as settled in her job as before and thought she needed to do extra work; her manager worked long hours and Joan thought that he might expect the same from her.

I asked Joan what had changed in the last couple of months and she told me that the only real change in her life was that her old boss, Peter, had moved divisions, and she now had a new boss called Michael. Joan said that Michael was a good hard-working manager and that she didn't have any problems with him. When I enquired further it appeared that the main differences between her two managers was that her old manager had given her lots of praise and reassurance for her work, whereas her new manager just got on with his job and left her to get on with hers in a similar fashion. Essentially, the upshot was that Michael didn't manage Joan on an emotional level. Michael's salary had a huge bonus component and he was working longer hours to enhance his wages, whereas Joan's wage was the same regardless of the hours that she worked. Joan didn't want to ask her new manager if everything was OK with her work as she thought that this may leave her in a weak position. As a result of this, she felt that she was never sure quite where she stood.

As Joan and I discussed some of her difficulties further, she was able to identify tension in her body as she talked about specific areas of her work. When we gently focused and became curious about Joan's tension we were able to identify two of her rules which turned out to be; 'If people are happy with me and appreciate me at all times, then I will be OK' and 'If I feel strong and in control of my emotions at all times, then I will be OK'. It appeared that the lack of obvious appreciation from Michael for her work, and Joan not really wanting to talk with Michael about her work performance had gradually begun to challenge her rules about others being happy with her and appreciating her.

The violation of this rule alongside Joan's other rule about being in control of her feelings had led to her over-controlling her emotions and hiding her sense of vulnerability. My hypothesis was that these factors working together had contributed to Joan becoming depressed. Joan felt exceptionally undervalued. She also had an experience of feeling lost and vulnerable. Joan's symptoms of depression and her concentration difficulties in particular were worrying her as she feared this could lead to her making mistakes and then losing her job. She went on to explain that she did not have children and to a large extent her work and her husband had become her life and the thought of losing her job made her feel suicidal.

Of course, Joan didn't realise that she was beginning to dig a bit of a hole for herself. It was an unfortunate consequence of trying to get back on track but being railroaded by her rules at the same time. Joan was on the verge of visiting her general practitioner, which would probably mean that she would be signed off from work for weeks. It appeared that she had unintentionally worked her way into a situation where she had the potential to dig herself deeper and deeper into a depressive position.

It would have been very difficult for Joan to see things as they really were when she was in her hole. When we fall into a metaphorical hole we have a natural human tendency to keep digging. Of course, to someone outside of the problem an obvious solution would be for Joan to allow herself to be vulnerable, talk to her manager about her struggles with coping, reduce her working hours to contracted levels and ask for regular reviews of her work. However, these seemingly obvious solutions would not have felt right to Joan due to the rigidity of her rules. Her main focus was on blaming herself: telling herself that it was her fault. It turned out that Joan's sense of well-being was completely dependent on somebody else praising her. This may be quite hard to fully understand just reading about it, but the connection between Joan's rule violations and the negative affect it had on her could not be understated.

'Has anyone asked Joan what she's doing
down there?'

Essentially, the main message that I try to get across to clients like Joan is that rules are developed by our brains to keep us safe. They are usually created early in our lives as children and may help us during that period of time. However, as we grow older, rules can become out of date and maladaptive. By maladaptive I mean that our rules can hold us back rather than work productively for us.

Joan's rule 'If people are happy with me and appreciate me at all times, then I'll be OK' may have helped her as a child. It may have helped her with her teachers at school or even with her parents, but when she was working for her new manager, this old rule became very unhelpful.

---

## Further exploration

If you would like to investigate what your rules are, begin by noticing what you expect from yourself and others. I have placed some examples of rules that some people expect of themselves and others at the end of this chapter (see Tables 12 & 13). The rule challenging exercise (see Table 14) that I have also included at the end of this chapter has been designed to bring the impact of your rules into your awareness. This exercise is not powerful enough on its own to change your rules, but it may make your rules slightly more flexible. Use the self (see Table 12) and others (see Table 13) rule lists to make a note of your rules. Rules about the self could be ideas such as, 'If others are happy with me at all times, then I will be OK'. Whereas, examples of rules about others may be, 'If people respect me and listen to me at all times, then I will be OK'.

When I first started having therapy I was a bit surprised when I found out how rigid my rules were. I kind of knew they were there in the background but I hadn't really given them much thought before therapy. As I have mentioned already, they were something along the lines of: 'If I produce results and I am contributing at all times, then I will be OK' and, 'If I meet the highest standards at all times, then I will be OK'. My rules meant that I spent most of my time working and not spending time with my family. If I wasn't working I felt as though something wasn't quite right. I found it difficult to stop and rest even for five minutes. If I stopped working I felt guilty or anxious. It felt wrong if I wasn't achieving.

It is often useful to notice the kinds of rules that can leave you feeling distressed, upset, anxious, guilty, or angry. Sometimes rules are difficult to recognise. Close friends and family members will help you to notice what your rules are if you ask them. I have put some of my rules below.

If when you read them you think that my rules made me particularly difficult to live with and work with, you would be correct. I tended to get irritated, anxious, and angry if my rules were broken, often making life difficult for others as well as myself.

'If nobody is upset with me and everybody likes me at all times, I will be OK'

'If I achieve at all times, then I will be OK'

'If I am in control at all times, then I will be OK'

'If I am strong at all times, then I will be OK'

'If people are happy with my performance, then I will be OK'

'If I am the best at what I do, then I will be OK'

'If people don't let me down, then I will be OK'

During the time when I struggled the most I took on very difficult tasks and generally worked until I became exhausted. When I wasn't able to work the way I did before I felt guilty about not working and started beating myself up over it. In therapy, when I thought about what was happening it really brought to my attention what I was doing. I thought I was doing all the extra work to help others and my family but obviously it didn't feel that way to them. Ironically, in my valiant attempts to prove to myself that I was OK I ended up upsetting most of the people that I came into contact with.

'Thanks for coming to see me to talk to me James. I couldn't help noticing that you like rules, so I made you these.'

## Where do our rules come from?

Sometimes it might be difficult to think about where your rules came from. To find out, fill out rule sheets on behalf of the people that brought you up. How would they have filled in their rule sheets? What made them anxious, angry, guilty, or sad? Once you have completed this exercise you will have a pretty good idea about who you learnt your rules from. I filled in a rule sheet on behalf of my father, gauging his reaction to events. Interestingly, we had practically the same rules apart from one or two.

Table 12. Rules for the self

| Rule sheet: Use the box to the right to note which rules apply to you | ✔ |
|---|---|
| If I am in control at all times, then I will be OK | |
| If people are happy with me at all times, then I will be OK | |
| If I do things perfectly at all times, then I will be OK | |
| If I am the best at what I do at all times, then I will be OK | |
| If I don't experience any unusual bodily sensations, then I will be OK | |
| If I am feeling good at all times, then I will be OK | |
| If I am feeling confident at all times, then I will be OK | |
| If I am not blamed for things, then I will be OK | |
| If I show dominance at all times, then I will be OK | |
| If I perform well at all times, then I will be OK | |
| If I am physically well at all times, then I will be OK | |
| If I am assertive at all times, then I will be OK | |
| If I know what I am doing at all times, then I will be OK | |
| If I know what is going to happen at all times, then I will be OK | |
| If I appear to others as though I know what I am doing, then I will be OK | |
| If I feel safe at all times, then I will be OK | |
| If I appear competent at all times, then I will be OK | |
| If I show no signs of vulnerability, then I will be OK | |
| If I am in control of my feelings at all times, then I will be OK | |
| If I say 'Yes' to all requests at all times, then I will be OK | |
| If I am strong at all times, then I will be OK | |
| If things go wrong it is all my fault | |
| If I don't let people down, then I will be OK | |
| If I can fix things, then I will be OK | |
| If I am in control of my body at all times, then I will be OK | |
| Total number of rules endorsed (write total number of rules endorsed in right-hand column) | |

Table 13. Rules for others

| Rule sheet: Use the box to the right to note which rules apply to you | ✔ |
|---|---|
| If others don't challenge me, then I will be OK | |
| If people are happy with me at all times, then I will be OK | |
| If people around me don't make any mistakes, then I will be OK | |
| If others tell me that I am the best at what I do at all times, then I will be OK | |
| If people around me are happy, calm and relaxed, then I will be OK | |
| If people around me are polite and respectful, then I will be OK | |
| If people around me are confident, then I will be OK | |
| If others don't criticise me, then I will be OK | |
| If others let me take charge, then I will be OK | |
| If people around me appreciate me, then I will be OK | |
| If people around me tell me that I am alright, then I will be OK | |
| If people listen to me at all times, then I will be OK | |
| If people around me know what they are doing at all times, then I will be OK | |
| If others reassure me, then I will be OK | |
| If others show confidence in me at all times, then I will be OK | |
| If others help me feel safe, then I will be OK | |
| If others approve of me at all times, then I will be OK | |
| If others show no signs of vulnerability, then I will be OK | |
| If others put my needs ahead of their own, then I will be OK | |
| If others say "Yes" to my requests when I ask them, then I will be OK | |
| If I am around strong people, then I will be OK | |
| If others take the blame for mistakes, then I will be OK | |
| If others don't let me down, then I will be OK | |
| If others can fix things for me, then I will be OK | |
| If others are there for me when I need them, then I will be OK | |
| Total number of rules endorsed (write number of rules endorsed in right-hand column) | |

## My Rule Sheet

For example, If I am strong and in
control, then I will be OK

If I am...................................................
then I will be OK

If I am...................................................
then I will be OK

If I am...................................................
then I will be OK

If I am...................................................
then I will be OK

If I am...................................................
then I will be OK

**My Rule Sheet**

For example, If others like me at all
times, then I will be OK

If others..............................................
then I will be OK

If others..............................................
then I will be OK

If others ..............................................
then I will be OK

If others..............................................
then I will be OK

If others..............................................
then I will be OK

Table 14. Rule challenging exercise

## Rule challenging exercise

**Rule** If others are happy with me, then I will be OK.

**How real and familiar does the rule feel?**

It feels real a lot of the time. It feels as though it is part of me.

**What impact does the rule have on your life?**

A lot of my goals are focused on things I need to do to keep other people happy.

It makes me easy to manipulate and once people realise I am like that they will often use it to make me feel bad so that I will do what they want.

**What benefits does this rule have on your life?**

Generally, most people seem to be unhappy with me at some point so I guess it just makes me feel miserable.

**Were you born with that rule?**

No.

**How old is the rule?**

I guess about 40 years old.

**Where do you think the rule came from?**

I learnt it from my parents.

**If you learnt the rule from a person, where do you think he or she learnt it from?**

I think my parents learnt it from their parents. It seems to be stronger on my father's side of the family.

**Do you want to keep that rule?**

Definitely not.

**If you gave yourself an opportunity to have another rule, what rule would you pick?**

Other people are responsible for their own happiness. I am responsible for my happiness. I can help others, or give advice to others, but they are responsible for their own feelings.

**How do you think you might feel if you choose to believe your new rule as much as the old one?**

I would feel as though I am not continually failing to please others. I would feel more relaxed.

**How does knowing that you can choose to have another rule make you feel?**

It feels a little alien. It feels a little hard-hearted. But, I feel better because I know logically this will create less stress and I will feel better and it will actually be more beneficial to others in the long-term.

## Rule challenging exercise

| Rule |
| --- |

**How real and familiar does the rule feel?**

**What impact does the rule have on your life?**

**What benefits does this rule have on your life?**

**Were you born with that rule?**

**How old is the rule?**

**Where do you think the rule came from?**

**If you learnt the rule from a person, where do you think he or she learnt it from?**

**Do you want to keep that rule?**

**If you gave yourself an opportunity to have another rule, what rule would you pick?**

**How do you think you might feel if you choose to believe your new rule as much as the old one?**

**How does knowing that you can choose to have another rule make you feel?**

# Advice from the Black Dog

If you find that you are in situations where your rules are violated on a regular basis you will start to feel emotionally run down after a while. When this occurs you can either change your environment so that less of your rules are broken, or you could consider changing your rules or making them more flexible. When you start to get the balance right I will be very grateful and I will be on my way.

# CHAPTER 12

# Limiting beliefs

In 1967 the psychiatrist Aaron T. Beck summarised his ideas about belief systems in individuals with depression. In one of his major works: *Depression: Clinical, experimental, and theoretical aspects*, he described a negative belief triad, that included beliefs about the self, others, and the world.

Generally speaking, limiting beliefs are deeply held ideas about ourselves that we fear are true. By the time that we become adults, our beliefs can become so set within us that we feel that they are part of who we are. We may also carry out numerous 'safety behaviours' to protect ourselves from them without being aware of it. Most of us have absolutely no idea that our beliefs are in total control of our lives.

I discovered that one of my limiting beliefs was: 'I am a failure!' The funny thing about it was no matter how hard I worked or how much I achieved, the belief 'I am a failure' was always still there. It seemed like what I had done in the past counted for nothing. Trying to prove the belief wrong demanded so much of my time that it affected my health and the happiness of my family. I didn't realise it was driving me so much. I didn't feel in control of my life. It drove me to do more and more. I didn't really know how to stop!

My therapist helped me to notice that in many situations I was experiencing high levels of painful emotions that were inconsistent with the situation that I was faced with. For example, we identified that I had an over the top reaction to even small amounts of criticism. Using this awareness my therapist helped me to recognise that the belief 'I am a failure' which was experienced at a 'felt sense level' was the main driver for my emotional reaction. My extreme distress response was the primitive part of my brain trying to protect me from being a failure. After this, I became much more observant and aware of my emotional reactions (without judging them) and I usually took a minute out to see if a limiting belief was influencing me. When I became distressed my thinking may have gone something along the lines of: 'That's interesting! I'm experiencing really intense feelings right now, but I haven't actually done anything wrong and nothing is going to happen to me. What am I possibly stuck with right now or believing about myself that is making me feel this way?'

'James! Do you think you might be trying to do too much again?'

## How do we develop limiting beliefs?

The most obvious ways that we develop limiting beliefs do not really need any scientific evidence or scientific explanation. If parents or caregivers tell their children that they are stupid, worthless, or a failure it is purely logical that most children will develop limiting beliefs! Most of us would understand that children treated in this way would develop a negative view of themselves. In a similar manner, children can develop limiting beliefs through negative messages from caregivers that are implied through action and inaction. Once a child develops limiting beliefs they are usually very difficult to shift and are retained into adulthood.

There are also other ways in which people develop beliefs: ways we might not normally think about. I am saying this because I have come across a large number of clients who appear to have limiting beliefs, yet they cannot recall any significant trauma, and they have no history of parental abuse or poor treatment as a child.

### The subtle ways that we develop beliefs

In 2014, researchers from the University of Michigan, Jacek Debiec and Regina Sullivan completed some interesting research on rats. They taught young female rats to fear the smell of peppermint by pumping the smell of peppermint into their cages and giving them electric shocks at the same time. The female rats were then left to their own devices for a while, mated, became pregnant, and gave birth. After the mothers had given birth, researchers re-exposed the mother rats to the peppermint smell again, without electric shocks this time, while they were with their young. The researchers found that infant rats learned to fear the peppermint smell by noticing the scent of fear given off by their mothers. Brain scans carried out on the baby rats revealed that a fear of peppermint was programmed directly into the infant rats' amygdala. As I wrote about earlier, the amygdala is the seat of our natural response to threat. There is growing evidence that infant children's brains operate in a similar way to baby rats' brains, both in the womb and after birth up until the age of six months: research is still in progress.

Research findings such as those described above are beginning to suggest at a most basic level that children absorb their parents' fears. The implication here is that we are biologically pre-programmed to accept a rapid transfer or download of information from our parents. One of the reasons why Jacek Debiec set up his experiments in the first place was because he had come across many people who were coming to him with nightmares and post-traumatic symptoms connected to the Holocaust. The issue that confused him most of all was that these particular adults with post-trauma symptoms had not even been born during the Holocaust; they were children of Holocaust survivors and somehow and someway they had absorbed the fears of their parents.

## Social learning and belief systems

The above methods of learning belief systems are not the only ways that we can develop belief systems. There is also a process called social learning that we will need to examine.

In 1977, Albert Bandura wrote about a process he identified in children called observational learning, which is now more commonly known as social learning theory: he witnessed that children act as little information processors watching and copying the behaviour of important others, or role models. For example, in the preface to this book I mentioned that my father felt that he needed to do things perfectly and to very high standards. It is a big possibility that I may have learnt this way of behaving from him. A further strong personal clue to this is the number of times my younger brother has told me, 'Jim! You know what your main problem is … You're just like DAD!'

## Identifying limiting beliefs

To identify limiting beliefs, therapists will usually start off by asking their clients to remember a situation where they experienced quite intense emotions. Clients determine if their emotion is more intense than they think is appropriate for the situation. Therapists then help their clients complete an exercise called a downward arrow. With a downward arrow exercise, therapists help their clients to keep following feelings and thoughts until their clients reach the deepest fears that they hold about themselves. I have put an example of a downward arrow exercise on the next page (see Figure 8a).

I strongly advise you not to do this exercise by yourself unless you have already completed therapy. I once showed one of my assistant psychologists (a psychologist in pre-doctoral training) how to complete a downward arrow for therapy purposes, but didn't expect her to go away and use it immediately. A few hours later she knocked on my door looking very agitated. She explained that she had practised a downward arrow on one of my other assistants, and that this other assistant was absolutely devastated, and had been crying for several hours non-stop. I then needed to go to see this other assistant to help her stay with her intense emotions: which is a common reaction when beliefs are activated. Luckily, I was able to assist her with a small amount of belief work.

**Downward arrow exercise**

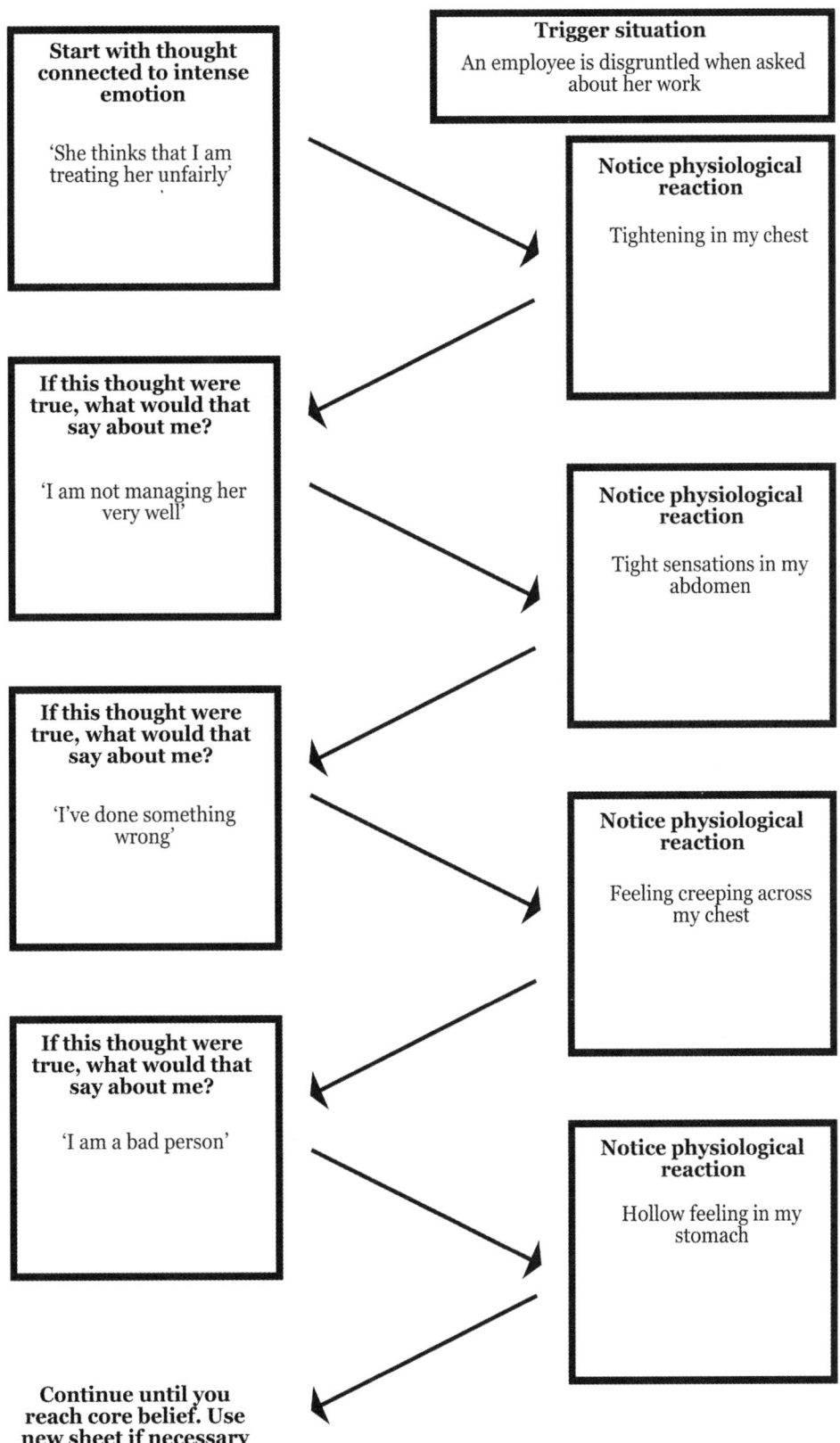

Figure 8. An example of a downward arrow exercise

## Downward arrow exercise

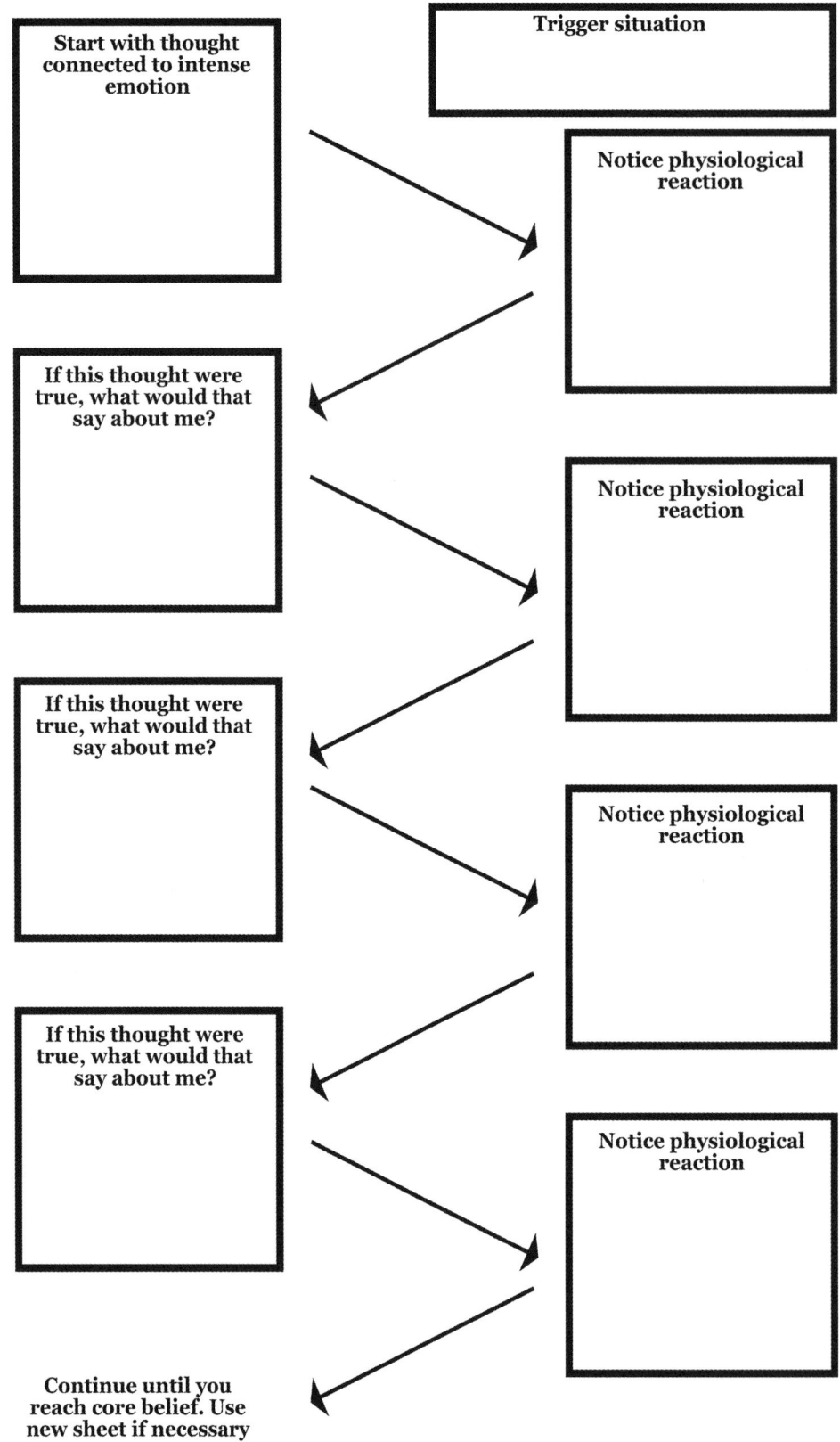

# Advice from the Black Dog

The best way to take away the power of limiting beliefs is to recognise that they are there. The definition of 'to believe' is – Accepting that something is true without evidence or proof.

While it can be understandably upsetting to initially identify limiting beliefs, it is another step in the direction of your recovery and freedom from ongoing pain, suffering and despair.

Before being able to let something go, we first need to know what we are holding onto. While we have no choice about beliefs being there in the first place, once we recognise them we can start to let them go, saying 'Thanks, but no thanks'.

## CHAPTER 13

# Drawing out simple cycles

I often draw out cycles using my whiteboard to explain how people's distressing feelings and behaviours are being maintained. I do this to help people recognise that some of the things they do tend to keep their problems in place. Once you realise that you have a cycle in place, you can then work out how to break the cycle.

The first part of noticing a cycle is making a connection between beliefs, rules, and safety behaviours. It generally looks something like Figure 9 (see across).

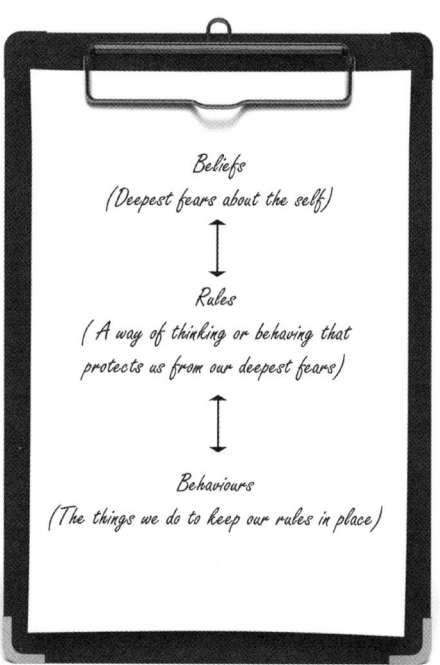

Figure 9. Beliefs, rules and behaviours

### What a cycle looks like

As I mentioned earlier one of my rules was, 'If I am successful at all times and if people are happy with my work at all times, then I will be OK.' The main things I did were to work very long hours, make sure I did everything perfectly, not take breaks, compare my work with others to make sure that I was the best, and got angry if anybody made suggestions about improvements. My therapist would have placed my information on a board that looked something like Figure 10.

My therapist asked me what happened when I felt I could not keep to my rule of being successful at what I did at all times. I told her this made me feel highly anxious and on-edge. We worked out that I was getting these feelings because my belief: 'I am a failure' was being activated when I was not maintaining my rule. When this happened, I felt that I needed to do what I was doing before even more, to protect myself from my fear of being a failure. This led to me working even harder. Eventually, I worked so hard that I became exhausted.

My therapist asked me about how my very best attempts at proving to myself that I wasn't a failure, may have actually ended up with me believing that I was a failure even more. It's a bit obvious when I describe it now because I'm not in the cycle, but my partner was unhappy with me and my kids were upset because I was working so much. My life felt like a mess and I felt that I was failing in all areas of life.

My therapist would have drawn diagram's not unlike Figures 11 and 12 for me to look at.

I have left a blank sheet at the end of this chapter. You can fill this in by yourself or you can complete it with a therapist, if you have one.

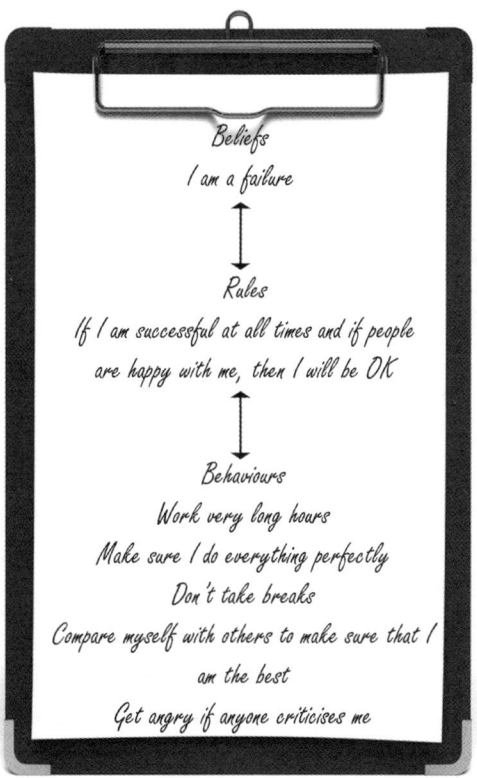

Figure 10. Completed beliefs, rules and behaviour diagram

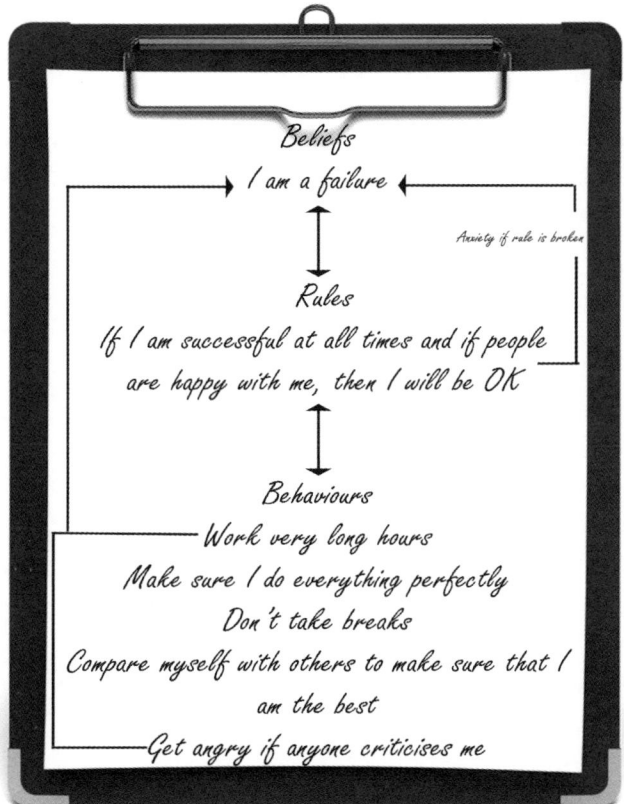

Figure 11. More advanced completed beliefs, rules and behaviour diagram

## Cycle of beliefs, rules and behaviours

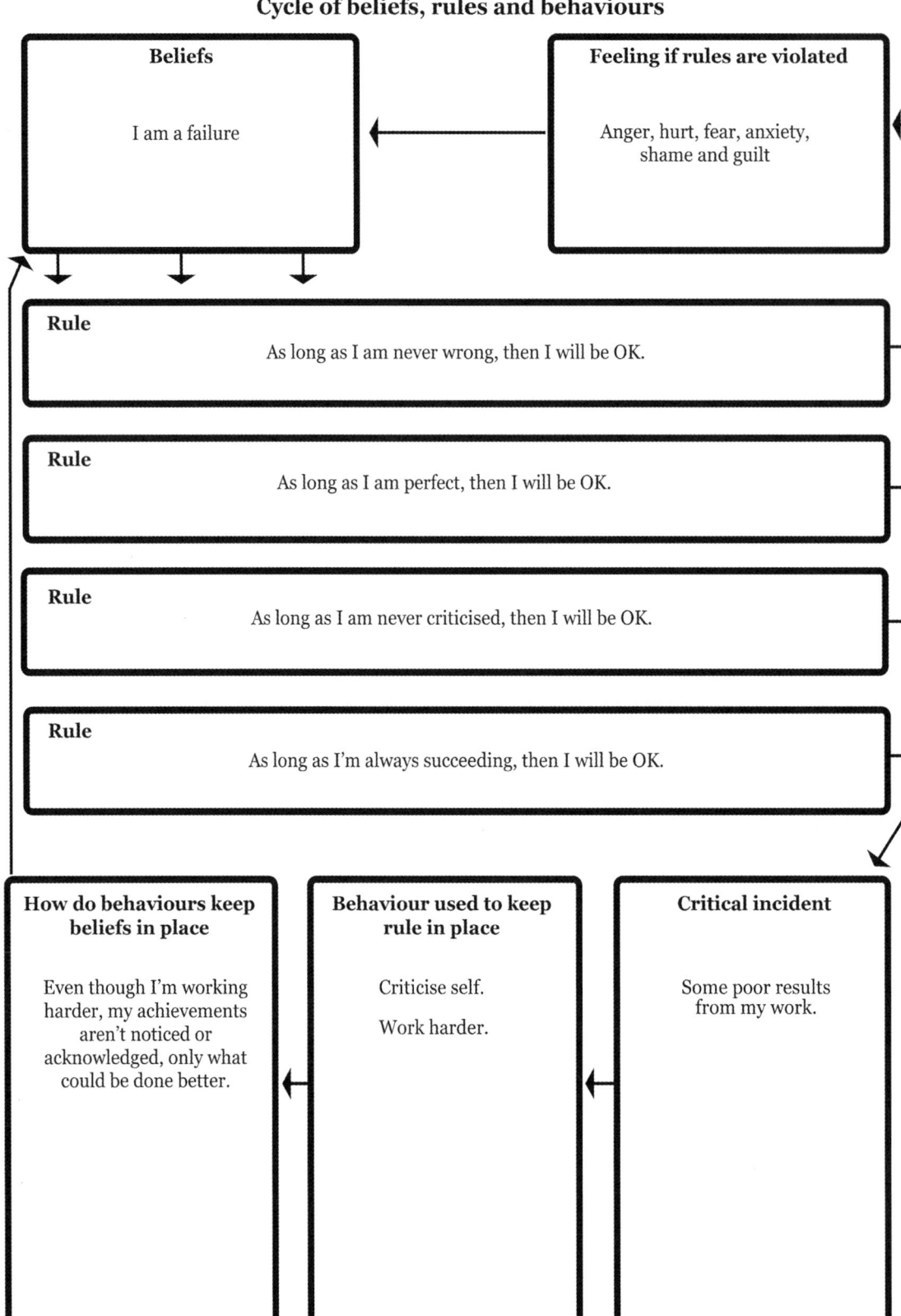

**Beliefs**

I am a failure

**Feeling if rules are violated**

Anger, hurt, fear, anxiety, shame and guilt

**Rule**

As long as I am never wrong, then I will be OK.

**Rule**

As long as I am perfect, then I will be OK.

**Rule**

As long as I am never criticised, then I will be OK.

**Rule**

As long as I'm always succeeding, then I will be OK.

**How do behaviours keep beliefs in place**

Even though I'm working harder, my achievements aren't noticed or acknowledged, only what could be done better.

**Behaviour used to keep rule in place**

Criticise self.

Work harder.

**Critical incident**

Some poor results from my work.

Figure 12.  Another example of a beliefs, rules
and behaviour diagram

## Cycle of beliefs, rules and behaviours

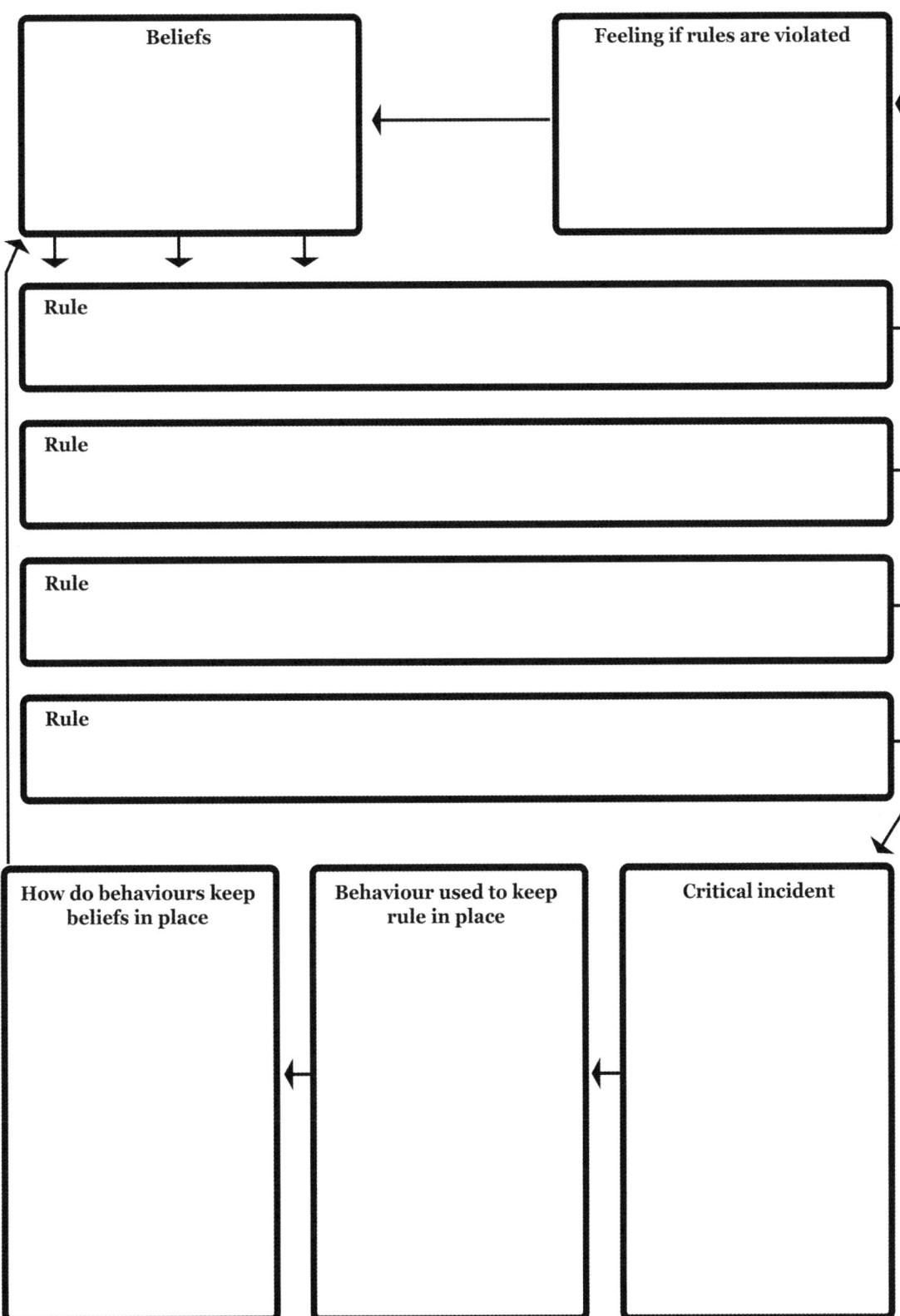

# Advice from the Black Dog

The connection between beliefs, rules, and behaviours may leave you feeling like a dog chasing its own tail. The best thing to do in this situation is to stop and notice what you are doing.

Beginning to see that you are chasing your own tail will help you appreciate that you are caught up in an unhelpful, self-defeating cycle. It's certainly not your intention to defeat yourself, it is an unfortunate consequence of being caught up in something that is familiar although not very pleasant.

## CHAPTER 14

# More cycles

Another common cycle is a thought, feeling, behaviour, and physiology cycle. In this cycle, thoughts influence feelings, feelings influence behaviour, and behaviour reinforces thoughts. The whole process works something like a downward spiral.

I will give you an example as it will make a lot more sense that way. A while ago, I worked with a lady called Vera who had been depressed for a short while. She worried a lot about what others thought of her and deep down inside she had fears that she was weak and incapable. She had a voluntary job in her local village shop for a couple of hours a week which had previously given her a lot of satisfaction. She 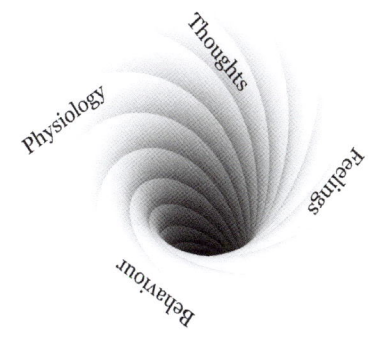 had enjoyed this job in the past because it had been an opportunity for her to catch up with the local villagers and find out what had been going on in her neighbours' lives. On one particular day she was pondering whether she might phone up and cancel her stint in the shop. She was thinking about this because she hadn't quite been herself due to her symptoms of depression and was concerned about what others might think of her. I have drawn Vera's thoughts, feelings, physiology, and behaviour cycle, (see Figure 13).

**Breaking cycles**

A cycle can be broken by directing attention to any one area of the cycle. This is because each part of a cycle is dependent on other parts of it to keep it in place. For example, if avoidant behaviour is challenged it creates fewer opportunities to mull over negative thoughts. If feeling sad is soothed away there is less tendency to mull over negative thoughts. If negative thoughts are challenged or dampened there is less intense emotion. It is hard for the cycle to maintain itself if pieces of it are missing. Later on I will offer more information about breaking patterns like this. A natural progression once cycles are identified is to work on goals, (see Table 15).

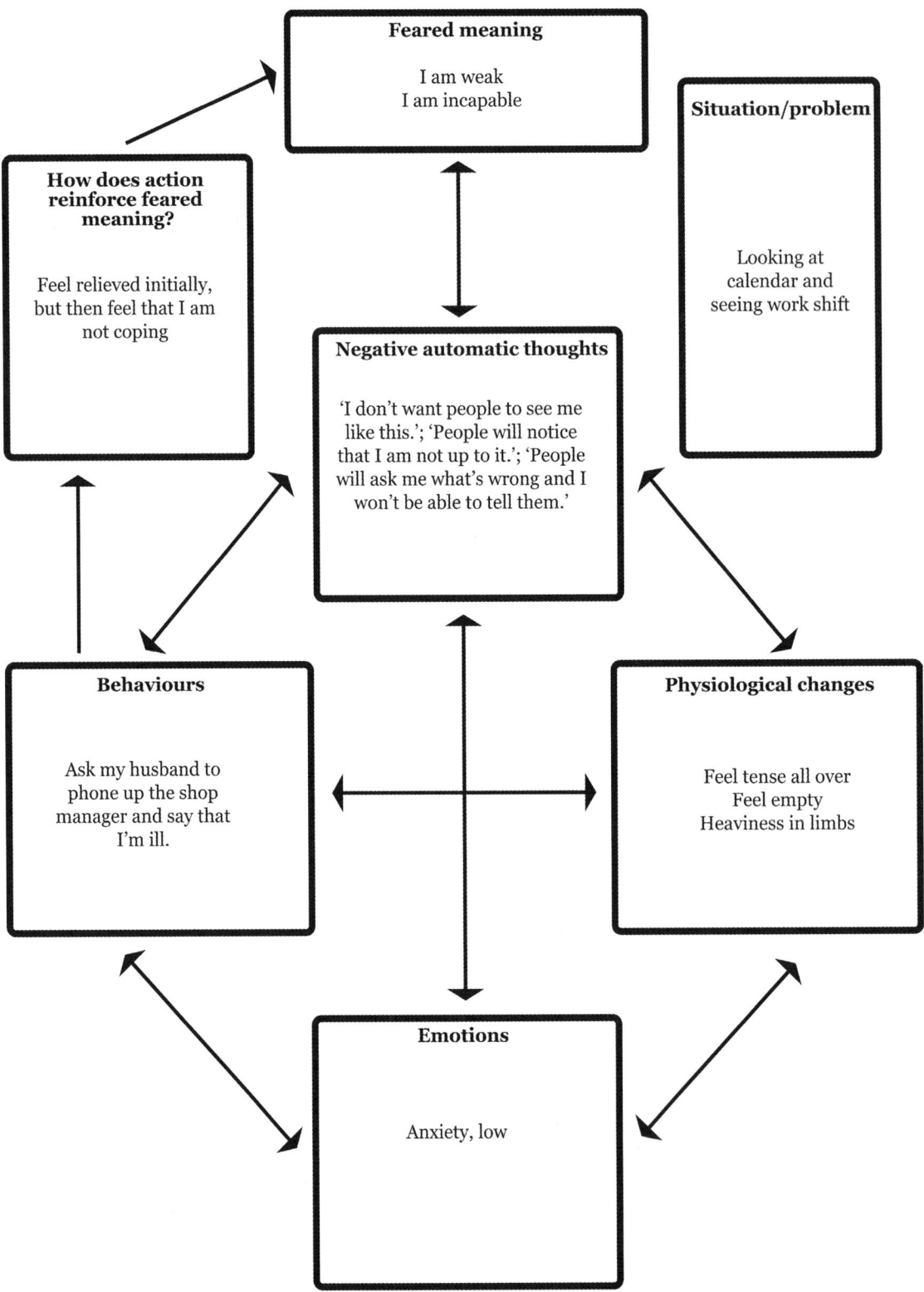

Figure 13. Vera's cycle

Table 15. Goal sheet example

## Old cycle/new cycle

| Past | Future |
|---|---|
| **Old beliefs** | **New beliefs** |
| 'I am incompetent' | 'I am OK' |
| 'I am not likeable' | 'I am me' |
| 'I am insignificant' | 'I am free' |
| ↓ | ↓ |
| **Old rules** | **New rules** |
| If I am in control of my environment at all times, then I will be OK. | It's normal to tell people how I feel. |
| If others like me at all times, then I will be OK. | It's OK to assert my needs. |
| If I am in control of my feelings at all times, then I will be OK. | It's important that I make room for my feelings. |
| If others notice my achievements at all times, then I will be OK. | It's OK to make mistakes as long as I learn from them. |
| ↓ | ↓ |
| **Old behaviours** | **New behaviours** |
| Keep feelings to self. | Tell others how I feel. |
| Check and double check everything. | Assert myself when I want to do something. |
| Try to predict problems before they happen. | Share problems with trusted others. |
| Keep problems to myself. | Check things once or just a few times. |
| Say "Yes" to all requests. | Validate and accept my feelings. |
| Concentrate on getting everything correct. | Be myself. |

## Old cycle/new cycle

| Past | Future |
|---|---|
| **Old beliefs** | **New beliefs** |
| ↓ | ↓ |
| **Old rules** | **New rules** |
| ↓ | ↓ |
| **Old behaviours** | **New behaviours** |

# Advice from the Black Dog

A cycle can be broken by paying attention to any area of the cycle. Once you notice a cycle, it will give you an idea about what you will need to do to break it.

Your intention to break a negative cycle is what matters most. Doing things differently or responding to your feelings in an alternative way will be another step towards freeing yourself from a destructive, yet familiar pattern of being.

## CHAPTER 15

# How to complete a CBT cycle

Before you fill in a CBT cycle it is usually practical to have a completed thought diary ready, so that you have a range of negative automatic thoughts (NATs) to work with (see chapter on self-observation). A good place to start is to look through the thoughts in your diary and pick out a thought that produces the most distressing emotion.

Once you have selected a NAT, verbally repeat the NAT in your mind for a little while and then complete a body scan. A body scan will involve you focusing your awareness on your body, and noticing physiological changes and emotions that accompany the NAT. The meaning behind the NAT can be identified by asking yourself, 'If this thought were true, what would it say or mean about me?'

A CBT cycle can be especially useful in bringing to mind how self-fulfilling prophecies work (see Figure 14). This will then naturally lead on to the completion of a NAT challenging exercise, which will be covered in the next chapter. A self-fulfilling prophecy occurs when we spend a significant amount of time and effort trying to prevent something happening, but the very things that we do to stop it happening actually cause it to happen. A natural progression after identifying a cycle is to move onto breaking a cycle. A cycle can be broken by directing attention to any one area of a cycle.

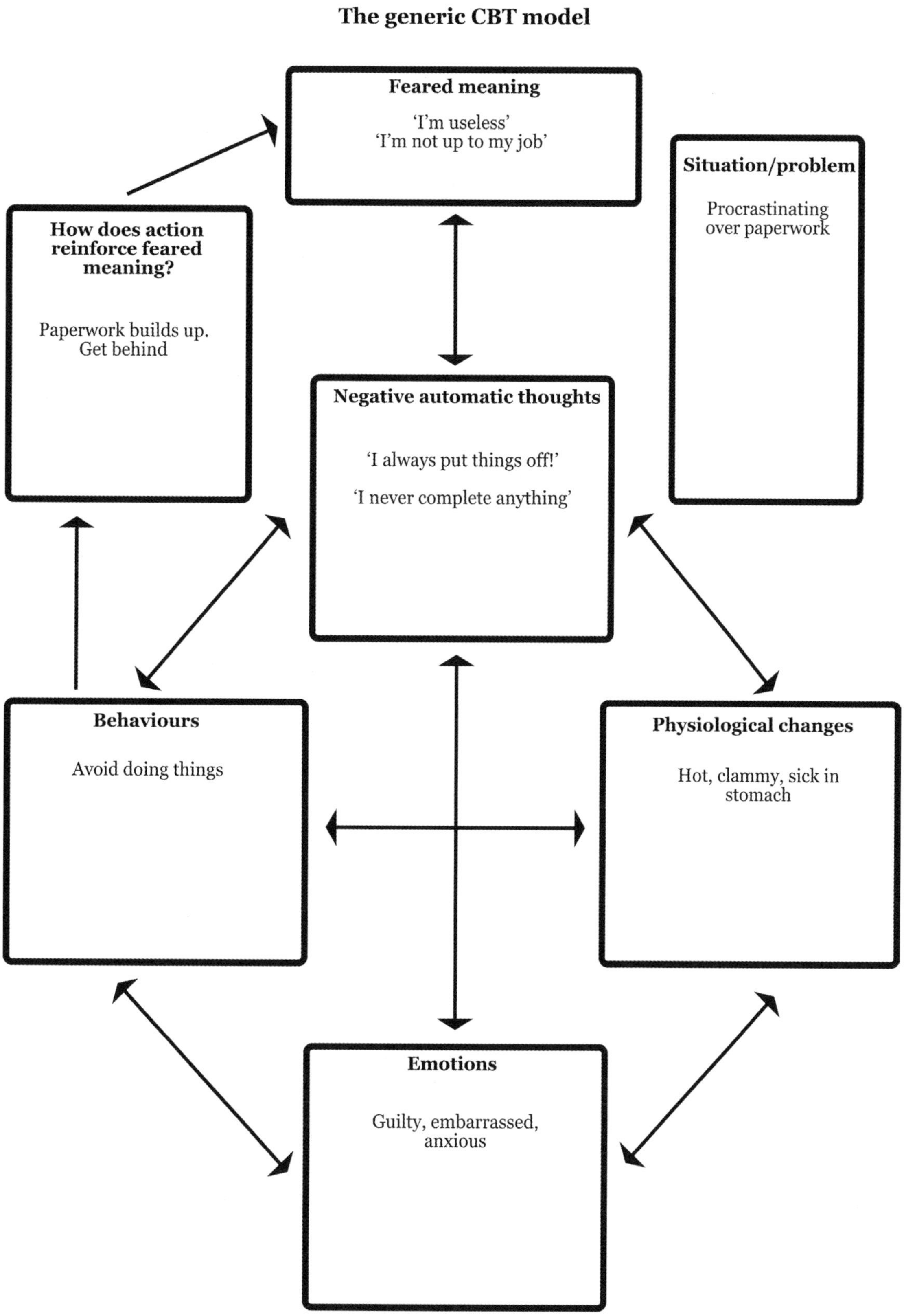

## The generic CBT model

**Feared meaning**

'I'm useless'
'I'm not up to my job'

**Situation/problem**

Procrastinating
over paperwork

**How does action
reinforce feared
meaning?**

Paperwork builds up.
Get behind

**Negative automatic thoughts**

'I always put things off!'

'I never complete anything'

**Behaviours**

Avoid doing things

**Physiological changes**

Hot, clammy, sick in
stomach

**Emotions**

Guilty, embarrassed,
anxious

Figure 14. An example of a negative cycle

## The generic CBT model

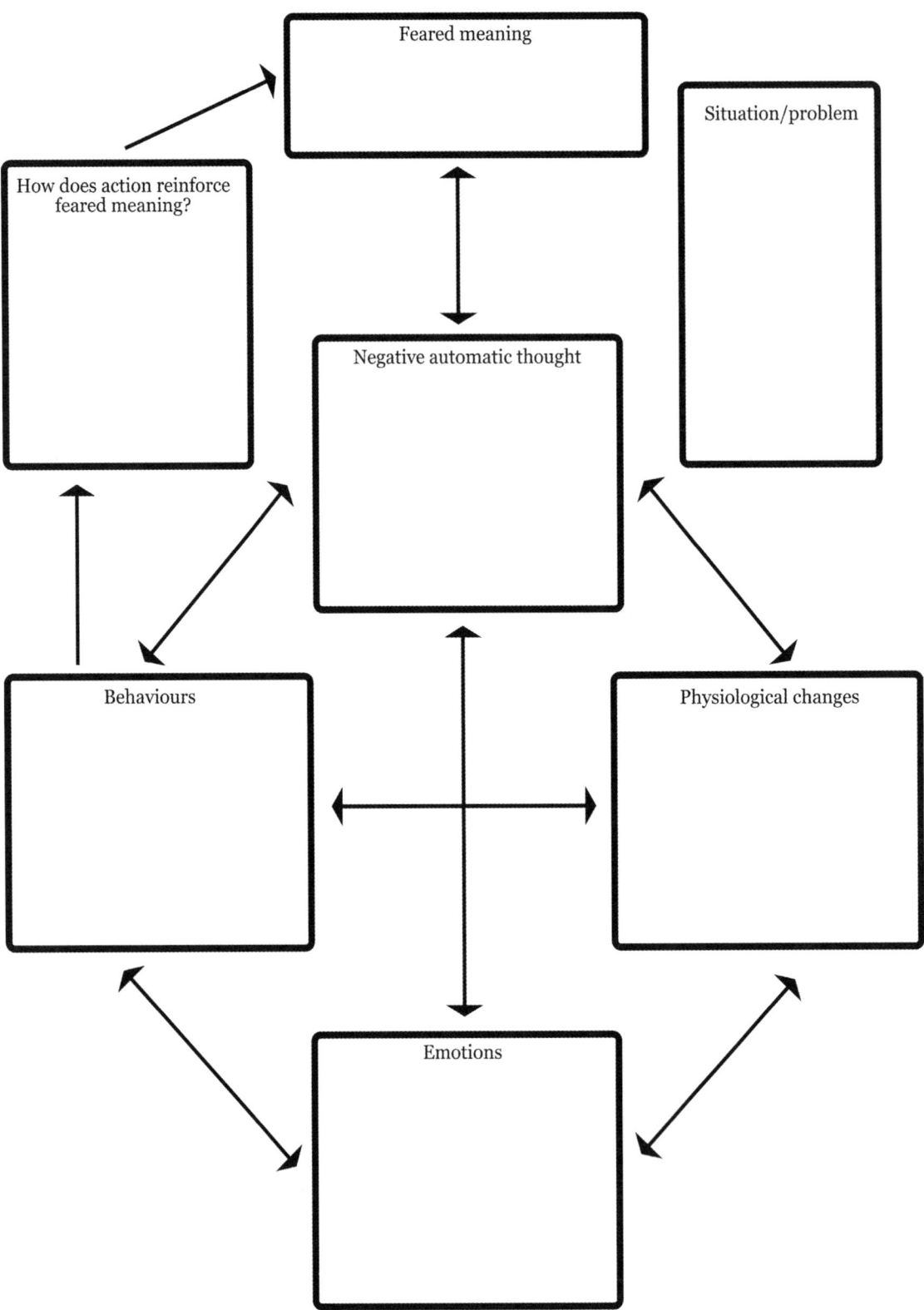

# Advice from the Black Dog

First, identify your negative automatic thoughts (NATs). Then complete a body scan to assess what is happening in your body when you have a NAT.

To obtain the meaning behind the NAT, ask yourself, 'What would it say about me if this were true?'

It's quite a skill learning to spot NATs. An important and helpful way to identify that NATs are present is to notice the persistent high levels of distress that comes with them. Your logical mind might also be telling you that the way you are feeling is excessive for the situation you are in.

## CHAPTER 16

# Challenging negative automatic thoughts

As I mentioned earlier, NATs are the types of thought that run in the back of our mind when we complete many day-to-day activities. More importantly, NATs are especially likely to be in operation for many individuals when they are feeling depressed or anxious. NATs are important to identify because they affect the way that we feel. Because of this, it will be very important for you to identify and challenge them as early as possible.

The first stage in recognising NATs is to set aside some time before or after events that provoke more intense emotions and write down the types of automatic thoughts that come to mind. Below, I have placed a list of common thoughts experienced by individuals with the Black Dog.

### Common automatic thoughts that concern the Black Dog

'No one likes me.'

'People would prefer if I'm not around.'

'I'm a burden.'

'I'm never going to be able to get out of this.'

'I haven't got anything to contribute.'

'This is completely pointless.'

'People won't notice if I don't go anyway.'

'Others will enjoy themselves without me.'

'People don't invite me anywhere.'

'They won't mind if I cancel, in fact they will be relieved.'

'I'll pull others down with me.'

## Common automatic thoughts that concern the Black Dog (cont.)

'Why does life always work out like this for me?'

'People are deliberately avoiding me.'

'No one ever likes me.'

'Why are others always better than me?'

## What do you do after you notice NATs?

Once you recognise that you have NATs you then have a choice about how you decide to react to them. You can either challenge them, or become aware of them and choose not to react to them. Many of my clients find that noticing their negative thoughts and choosing not to react to them is initially very difficult. With this in mind, I often find it useful in the early stages to spend time teaching my clients how to challenge their NATs.

One of the most effective ways to challenge NATs is to bring alternative explanations to mind. I have placed one type of thought challenging record on the next page (see Table 16) from one of my younger adult clients, Rebecca. A thought challenging record is really a collection of notes that you can make to provide alternative evidence against your NATs. You will find some empty tables at the end of this chapter that you can use to challenge your NATs. Negative automatic thoughts are placed in the first column, evidence for the automatic thoughts are placed in the second column, alternative explanations and more balanced thoughts in the third column, and the impact of challenging NATs is in the fourth.

To help my clients understand the power of NATs I often ask them to place their NATs into a CBT cycle. I have placed Rebecca's NAT into a CBT cycle, (see Figure 15). This makes the impact of the NAT a bit more obvious and explains why it is important to challenge them.

Table 16. An example of a NAT challenging form

## NAT challenging form

| Negative automatic thought, for example, 'Things aren't going to work out for me'. | Evidence for negative automatic thought, for example, 'I feel that it might happen'. | Evidence against negative automatic thought, for example, 'This has never happened before.' | New more balanced thought, for example, 'Although I feel panicky nothing has happened in the past and is unlikely to happen this time.' |
|---|---|---|---|
| 'John doesn't care about me!' | Things are just not moving forward. | John likes spending time me with. | I feel that things aren't moving forward, but the insecurity is coming from me not John. John seems happiest when he is with me. |
| | I feel that John doesn't love me anymore. | He seems very happy when he is with me. | |
| | There is something fundamentally wrong with me. | I am insecure about myself, this goes right back to my childhood. | |
| | John looks at other women. | John has asked me to spend time with him several times, but I have actually turned him down quite a lot. I push John away. | |
| | I don't feel attractive. | John rarely turns me down when I ask him to spend time with me. | |
| | John prefers to spend time with others than me. | | |

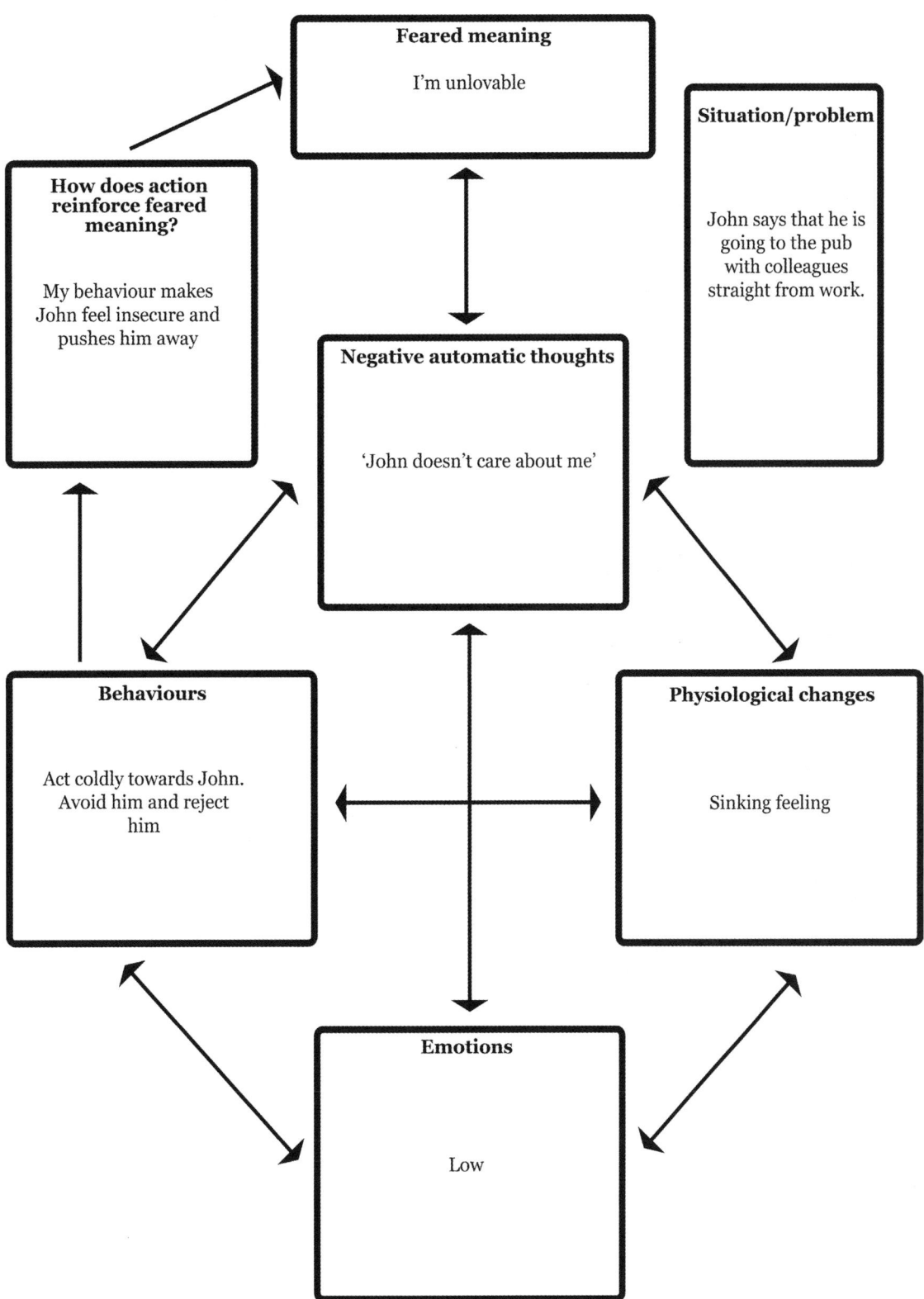

Figure 15. Example of a CBT cycle

## Completing thought challenging by yourself

Thought-challenging diaries can be incredibly useful to combat depression. Thought challenging is best used after you have drawn up a list of negative automatic thoughts (NATs), using a thought diary. Go through your list of NATs picking out thoughts that generate the highest degrees of distress. It is generally best to steer clear of using thought challenging exercises to work on beliefs. Beliefs, e.g., 'I am worthless' are better challenged with different types of exercises. Indeed, challenging beliefs with 'evidence for' and 'evidence against' can end up making you feel worse.

After you have selected a NAT write down as much evidence as possible to support your NAT. Using the analogy of a prosecution lawyer and a defence lawyer in a courtroom can be very useful to generate ideas. The evidence does not have to rely on facts, for example, evidence for the NAT, 'She is deliberately looking down on me' could be, 'I feel that it is true' or, 'I think it's true'. Move onto evidence against the thought only when evidence for the NAT is exhausted. Drawing attention to logical facts and thinking distortions can also be very useful when challenging NATs.

### Completing a NAT Challenging Form

Write down as much evidence for the NAT as possible. After you have written down your evidence for the thought, write down as much evidence against the thought as possible in the next column. After you have completed both columns, write down a more balanced thought. Once you have your balanced thought, run it through your mind and assess the way you feel emotionally and physically with this more accurate and balanced view.

I have placed an alternative version of a NAT challenging form on the next page. Table 17a is an example of a thought challenging form from an individual who fell out with a friend.

Once evidence for and against the NAT has been identified, come up with a more balanced thought that reflects both sides of the evidence. An example of a more balanced thought could be, 'I feel that she looks down on me, but in reality I don't know what she is really thinking, and she is probably behaving the way that she does because she is quite shy'.

**NAT challenging form**

| Negative automatic thought, for example, 'Things aren't going to work out for me'. | Evidence for negative automatic thought, for example, 'I feel that it might happen.' | Evidence against negative automatic thought, for example, 'This has never happened before.' | New more balanced thought, for example, 'Although I feel panicky nothing has happened in the past and is unlikely to happen this time.' |
|---|---|---|---|
| 'She thinks that I am treating her unfairly.' | She changed her mind about what we had agreed very suddenly. <br><br> I felt a negative vibe from her text. <br><br> I feel that she doesn't like me and thinks that I am a mean person. | She is out of her depth about what we agreed and is finding it difficult to manage. <br><br> Although she changed her mind she is still friendly and positive. <br><br> I cannot read people's minds and they have their own reasons for doing things that are not about me. <br><br> She has not said that she has been treated unfairly. | 'She changed her mind, and I have a habit of taking that kind of thing personally, but people have their own reasons for making their decisions that are nothing to do with me.' |

Collecting evidence against NATs can sometimes be difficult and because of this it will be important to persist. Some people find it helpful to complete NAT challenging exercises with a therapist. Alternatively, you might ask trusted loved ones to help you challenge NATs. You could also think about what you might say to others with similar NATs to yourself if you were helping them to challenge their NATs.

After completing a thought challenging record it is often useful to put the alternative more balanced thought into another CBT cycle and look at how it might change things, (see Figure 16 for Rebecca's positive maintenance cycle).

NATs often have a habit of coming back, so it may be useful for you to get your NAT challenging notes out and reread them when this occurs. In her book *Overcoming Social Anxiety and Shyness*, Professor Gillian Butler recommends the use of flash cards. Gillian Butler suggests that people make cards with their NATs on one side and place alternative more balanced thoughts on the other. Taking a small card out from time-to-time in various situations can then be used as a memory aid. Knowing the card is there without needing to look at it can also jog the memory. I have placed some blank positive CBT cycles at the end of this chapter for you to complete after you challenge NATs.

## NAT challenging form

| Negative automatic thought, for example, 'Things aren't going to work out for me'. | Evidence for negative automatic thought, for example, 'I feel that it might happen.' | Evidence against negative automatic thought, for example, 'This has never happened before.' | New more balanced thought, for example, 'Although I feel panicky nothing has happened in the past and is unlikely to happen this time.' |
|---|---|---|---|
| | | | |

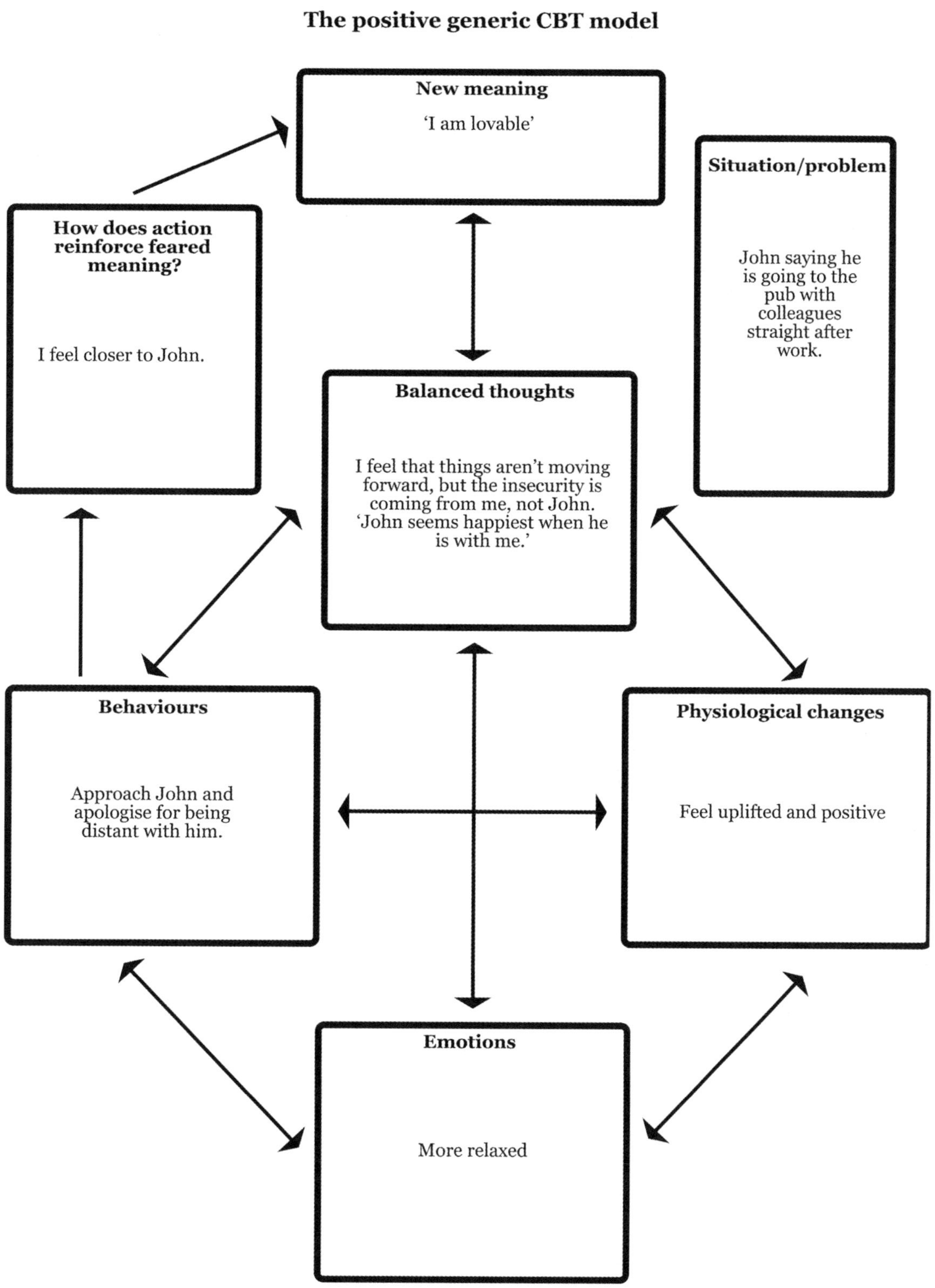

## The positive generic CBT model

**New meaning**

'I am lovable'

**Situation/problem**

John saying he is going to the pub with colleagues straight after work.

**How does action reinforce feared meaning?**

I feel closer to John.

**Balanced thoughts**

I feel that things aren't moving forward, but the insecurity is coming from me, not John. 'John seems happiest when he is with me.'

**Behaviours**

Approach John and apologise for being distant with him.

**Physiological changes**

Feel uplifted and positive

**Emotions**

More relaxed

Figure 16. Positive CBT maintenance cycle

## The positive generic CBT model

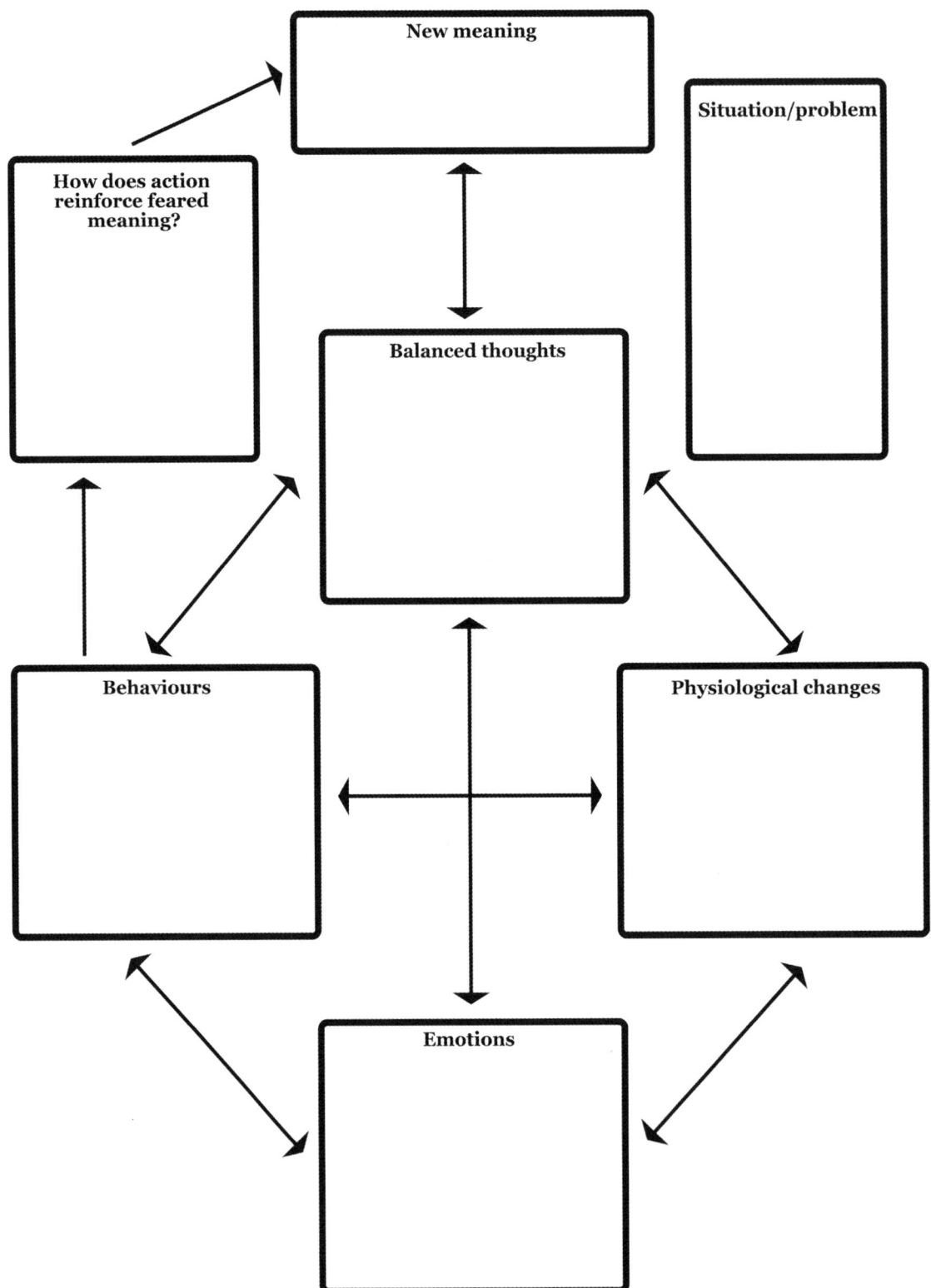

# Advice from the Black Dog

You will feel much better about yourself if you bring your negative automatic thoughts to mind, notice how they affect you, and then begin challenging them.

Initially, this is a time consuming process. However, it will be well worth the time, energy and attention you devote to it. You have undoubtedly spent or are spending your energy on other people or on other things. Choosing to make time for yourself to learn this new skill will be well worth it in the long run. NATs can be rather persistent and destructive intruders upon your wellbeing. Don't leave them unchecked.

## CHAPTER 17

# Approaching feelings

Emotional avoidance – also known as experiential avoidance – works as part of a cycle that keep problems in place for many people with depression. As such, it is very important that you consider approaching your feelings.

## Approaching low mood

Experiential avoidance – avoiding situations that produce feelings – often occurs quite automatically and habitually with depression, so using approach-based behaviour is not as easy as it might sound. The top part of the brain, the neocortex, probably recognises that in order to move on, it will be necessary to approach situations and spend more time with feelings. The subcortical mind (primitive mind), however, will tend to resist approach-based behaviour. As I mentioned in chapter 1, the subcortical mind does not learn readily through language, it learns best through experience (or experiential learning). With this in mind, one of the most helpful ways to teach the sub-subcortical mind new information is to create real life learning experiences. I will explain using an analogy.

## Frightened child analogy

I would like to invite you to think of the subcortical brain regions as a child who comes to your bedroom door one night feeling frightened. You ask the child what she is frightened of and she says that she thinks there is a monster in her wardrobe.

You have several options in terms of your response. Your first set of responses could be to ignore, rationalise, or avoid:

- You could tell the child not to be so silly and completely ignore her. The result of this is that the child waits around outside your room and continues to try to gain your attention. She could even wait outside your bedroom door all night.

- You could avoid the problem by telling the child that she can sleep in a bed in your room. The child is not scared anymore and happily gets into this bed. However, when the next day comes she seems more terrified than ever of sleeping in her own bedroom. Or you could use the following approach strategy:

- You could take the child's hand acknowledging that she feels really frightened and tell her that you are both going to look into the wardrobe together. When you approach the wardrobe the child is really scared and she tries to resist going towards it. You gently persist, telling the child that it really is OK to feel frightened. When you have opened the wardrobe door and you have both had a good look inside for a couple of minutes you notice that the child has become a lot less anxious and is happier to sleep in her own bed once more. You don't hear any more from the child that particular night.

With the last option you don't have to explain or rationalise, you simply help the child to acknowledge that she is scared. You confront the situation which you know logically is very low risk. In other words, you know there is a very low probability of there being a monster in her wardrobe. You then encourage her to find out for herself whether there is any danger. When this happens the

'Approaching the monster in the wardrobe'

child learns by her own experience. The primitive mind or subcortical region processes information in exactly the same way.

There is one more thing to note in this area. In our analogy, the child looking in the wardrobe will need to do this without carrying out any ritualistic behaviours or safety mechanisms. Such behaviours could include crossing fingers, closing her eyes, holding onto a teddy bear etc. If the child uses these things for reassurance then she will believe that her safety behaviours are keeping her safe and she will continue to rely upon them. Many people who experience mental health problems and emotional distress have safety behaviours, such as carrying diazepam, using beta-blockers, worrying, distracting themselves by listening to music, being with a safe person and so on. Using these safety behaviours will slow your progress and will hamper your experiential learning.

# Advice from the Black Dog

I understand that you may fear me, but approach me anyway. There is no one more loyal to you than me.

When you finally do approach me, you will know that I mean you no harm and never did.

When you bring yourself to me, you are letting me know that I am loved and cared for. You are telling me it is safe to feel hurt and sad. You are telling me I am allowed and not at fault.

CHAPTER 18

# Working with emotions

Often, feelings such as anxiety, guilt, and low mood are viewed as a threat, or are seen as bodily experiences that need to be feared or hidden. As a result, many people with the Black Dog use strategies such as ignoring feelings, controlling feelings, distracting themselves from feelings, hiding feelings, and using safety behaviours. This results in distress remaining high.

## You will begin to feel much better if you recognise how you are feeling

I spend a lot of time assisting my clients to notice they are having feelings because therapy works much more effectively when people are able to label their emotions. I generally start by gently encouraging my clients to begin observing what is happening in their body, and following this, help them to build a positive relationship with their feelings.

I have drawn a diagram (see Figure 17) that shows how many people react to their low mood. Figure 17 demonstrates the relationship between our natural attempts to control or avoid low mood and its impact on low mood levels. In my sessions I ask clients – 'What would happen if you tried the opposite of what you normally do? For example, instead of ignoring emotions, you notice them and tell them that it is fine for them to be there?'

'What if instead of distracting yourself from your low mood, you focus on your pain, and spend time in your body rather than in your head.'

I also ask – 'What would happen if you begin to see low mood as a friend rather than your enemy; if you allow your low mood to be visible rather than try to hide it and give permission

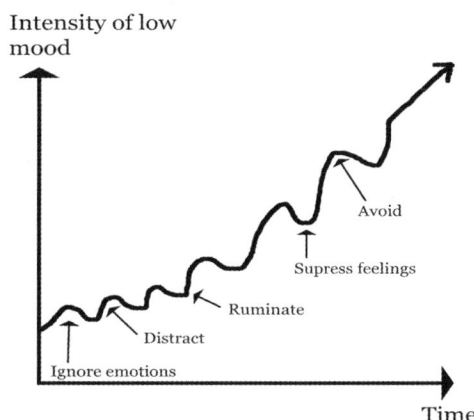

Figure 17. How people react to their low mood

92

for your low mood to stay, rather than trying to get rid of it as soon as possible?'

I often draw out a table on my whiteboard. I have reproduced a copy of it using Table 18.

The ideas covered in the right-hand column of Table 18 often confuse my clients, because the concepts feel so alien to them. It's not dissimilar to asking them to grab a red-hot poker, while assuring them that it is not going to harm them.

A counter-intuitive strategy to manage low mood is the last thing that most people who experience low mood would choose to do as they feel that their low mood will significantly worsen. By the way, when I say counter-intuitive I mean people carrying out behaviours or engaging in thoughts that are the direct opposite of what their intuition or feelings tell them is right.

| Common solutions to low mood | Strategy based on an opposites approach |
| --- | --- |
| Avoid uncomfortable feelings | Approach uncomfortable feelings |
| Distract self. Keep mind off of feelings | Focus on feelings |
| Perceive low mood symptoms as threatening. Fear them | Perceive low mood as part of the body that works for you. Embrace symptoms and allow symptoms to be visible |
| Control low mood, try to get rid of feelings as soon as possible | Allow low mood to stay for as long as it wants |
| Tell low mood that it shouldn't be there | Tell low mood that there are good reasons for it being there |

Table 18. A paradoxical approach to the Black Dog

In my personal experience, low mood is a very difficult emotion to accept. It can feel incredibly painful, and it does not dissipate very quickly. Accepting it can feel like you are opening up a bottomless void with no end to what it can take in. Low mood works with a bit of time lag, accepting it today often results in an improved mood the following day.

## An effective way to approach accepting feelings

If you remind yourself of the ideas covered in the early part of this book, you will remember that the neocortex is at the top of the brain, the prefrontal cortex is directly underneath that, and the subcortical regions are at the base of the brain. A slight problem with people who become highly distressed is that their prefrontal cortex tends to go offline when they are feeling most distressed. If this happens to you, you could find yourself in situations, where you are upset, where your mind goes blank, where you find it very difficult to think clearly or rationally, and you feel unable to complete exercises in this book.

With this in mind, I suggest that a very useful starting point is to begin viewing yourself as a bit like a parent to the subcortical or primitive regions of the brain. Imagine these parts of the brain not as the enemy but more like a servant that has worked for you loyally and tirelessly in the background, a servant who is also very rarely appreciated for his or her effort.

The best place to start your new parenting approach will be when you are on your own and when your distress levels are mild. Mild distress may be

'I've got a niggling feeling that Madam's not very happy with me'

around when you have day-to-day problems, for example, a problem at work, a problem with a friend or relative etc. Mild distress may also be around when you worry, or when you ask 'What if?' questions. The essence of the approach is to become more aware of your feelings, especially painful feelings at the earliest stage possible.

The best way to explain this is with a demonstration. Below I've illustrated how a conversation might develop with a client. In this example, the emotion I have selected to demonstrate is aggitation.

## A conversation about feelings

James: OK, Jemma, I would just like you to think of a problem that you have had just recently, a problem that when you think about it now, still leaves you feeling slightly aggitated.

Jemma: OK, I've thought of something. Do you want me to talk to you about it?

James: No, I'd like you to keep it to yourself for now. I'd just like you to think about where in your body you feel your emotion the strongest.

Jemma: I feel it most in my chest!

James: Good. Keep your focus there. Now place one of your hands on your chest in the place where you feel your emotion the strongest. You are placing your hand on your body where your emotion is, because many of us who are prone to avoiding emotions unconsciously and automatically move away from feeling emotions, and go into our heads or analytical mode instead. You are gaining a connectionwith your emotions and keeping your focus on how you are feeling.

Placing your hand on the part of your body where you feel your aggitation the strongest will also act as a reminder to you to keep your focus on your emotions. It is very important while you are doing this exercise to focus on feeling your feelings and remind yourself that you really are willing for your emotions to be there, even if you don't quite believe it at first.

Focusing on the part of your body underneath your hand with your mind, examine exactly what your emotion feels like. For example, how much space do your feelings take up? How painful or uncomfortable are your feelings. Jemma, can you rate the intensity of your feeling between 1 and 10, where 10 is the highest level?

Jemma: They're about a 7 at the moment.

James: OK, while you continue to feel your aggitation, mentally give it your permission to take up the space that it is taking up in your body. Taking things a little further, I would also like you to speak internally with your anxiety saying something along the lines of the following: 'Thank you for being there' ... 'There are very good reasons for you being there.'

Keep in mind the idea that from the primitive minds point of view there is a good reason for your aggitation being there, even if it does not make sense logically.

Now follow that by saying 'You are welcome to stay here for as long as you want'.

Bear in mind again Jemma, from the primitive mind's point of view that if it notices potential threat during its screening process, which may be physical or psychological, it is just doing its job properly if it brings that threat to your attention and helps you to prepare. The threat does not need to be logical, real or valid in the current time mode. If it has been perceived as a threat in the past, or you have previously confirmed the existence of the threat by withdrawing from it in the past, then from the primitive mind's point of view the threat is still active.

While feeling your symptoms of aggitation it is important when you speak to your feelings that you really mean what you are saying. Let go of all your thoughts and focus on your feelings. The importance of your self-talk is not in the words that you use but rather the intention behind your words. Keep in mind the idea of acceptance, recognition, of being grateful and being patient. I'm just going to ask you to do this for a minute Jemma and we will see what happens.

…a minute passes…

James: What do you notice at the moment Jemma?

Jemma: The feeling is going down…It's about a 4 now.

James: OK, staying with the feeling, noticing that it is going down. Just stay with it. We'll see what happens in another minute or so.

…another minute passes…

James: OK, Jemma what do you notice now?

Jemma: It's gone!

---

## Learning how to stay with your feelings

I'd just like to complete a short recap now. It is important in the early stages of this exercise that when you are experiencing aggitation, low mood, guilt, and anger that you practise being with your feelings as much as possible. This will help you in two ways. Firstly, it will help you to fear your feelings less, and secondly it will make it more likely that you will be able to use your acceptance approach when you are experiencing higher levels of distress. You will need to bear in mind that in a state of heightened distress the frontal lobes – where most of our logical thinking occurs – stop working somewhat. Practising acceptance over and over again when you are not so distressed will make it more likely that you will be able to access and use this approach more easily when you need it.

## The basal ganglia kicks in when we feel distressed

When we become highly distressed we are likely to continue to return to our old, unhelpful, habitual behaviours due to the strong influence of the basal ganglia which is located in the subcortical region of our brain. Activation of the basal ganglia results in us doing the same things that we have always done before. To change unhelpful habits, you will need to practise using your new positive habits – learned through CBT exercises – over and over again. Eventually, your new CBT habits will come into place automatically when you are faced with distressing situations. This process takes time, however, as brain wiring in the basal ganglia doesn't grow instantaneously.

# Advice from the Black Dog

Be compassionate towards me. Show the same compassion towards me that you so skillfully give to others in need.

When you show empathy for me I will stop hurting so much. My wounds will start to heal and my pain will be soothed away. Your compassion nourishes me and feeds my recovery.

## CHAPTER 19

# Breaking patterns of rumination

Most people who experience depression spend a significant portion of their time ruminating or worrying. Because these processes tend to maintain emotional difficulties it is important to break these habits.

## What is rumination?

Rumination is a process of churning negative thoughts over in one's mind. Most ruminative thoughts are connected to the self and the past. Some people suggest that rumination is useful because it can help to create lots of possibilities and can offer solutions when we are faced with specific problems. Rumination, however, does not work well when we try to analyse our way out of low mood.

A process of rumination is kept in place by the questions we ask ourselves; for example, if we ask, 'Why does this keep happening to me?' or 'What's wrong with me?' The questions that we ask ourselves throw up answers which, in turn, can lead us to ask more questions. Before long, if this process continues, we can end up having thoughts that appear to confirm our worst fears: for example, that we are worthless, wrong, useless, bad, and so forth. The irony of the whole process is that in our search for ways to avoid current or future painful feelings by ruminating, we end up dwelling on the past, and we can end up feeling worse than ever. It's not dissimilar to using a shovel to dig ourselves out of a hole. The more we dig, the deeper the hole gets! The problem is that often we do not feel that we have any other way of solving our problems, so we continue to use the same strategy, even though we know it doesn't work.

## How is worry similar or different to ruminating?

Worry is similar to ruminating in that it is also a process of thought churning. The main difference is that worry is focused on the future and potential outcomes. When people worry they think about upcoming situations and ask questions such as, 'What will I do if this happens?'; 'What is the worst thing that could happen?'; or 'What if this happens?' They do this because they think that if they can imagine the worst case scenario, then they will be able to put things in place

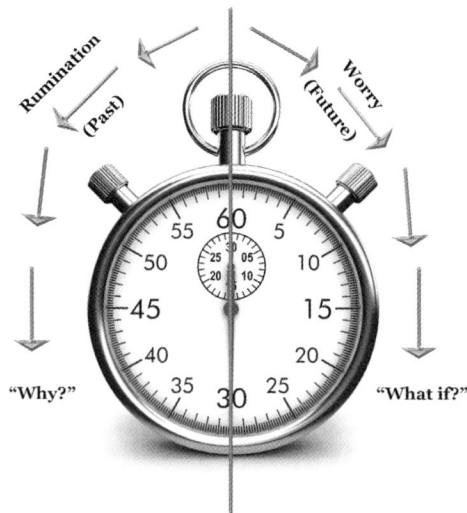

Rumination is thought churning about the past, worry
is thinking about what could go wrong in the future.

to deal with whatever happens in a particular situation. They think if they can
work out what might happen in advance then they will be able to cope better.

## The conscious mind

Most of us are aware that we have a conscious mind. We recognise that we
are conscious when we are awake to the thoughts, images, or sensations that we
experience. Information does not stay long in consciousness and, as such, the
conscious mind could be thought of as a whiteboard that begins to erase what is
written on it after only a few seconds. If you imagine your thoughts are like ink
on the whiteboard, you will notice that the ink or information expressed using
it, disappears so rapidly, the only way to keep anything on this whiteboard is to
continuously write on it over and over again. When new information is written
on the whiteboard, the previous information on the whiteboard disappears even
more rapidly. A further point you may note is that the amount of information
that can be written on the whiteboard at any one point in time is limited due to
the whiteboard's small size. I'll demonstrate how this works by referring to an
exercise that I completed with a client of mine called Jemma.

## Client exercise

James: Jemma, before we start I just want to let you know that this is not a test.
It's just a little exercise so that you can find out how much information your
mind can hold onto. I am going to start by asking you to remember five random
numbers and letters. Are you ready?

Jemma: Yes

James: 5A3KQ. Have you got that?

Jemma: Yes. I think so!

James: Alright, I now want you to remember these numbers as well. 27KR1...
Right Jemma, can you repeat that sequence for me?

Jemma: 27KR1

James: Good...And, the first sequence.

Jemma: ...Erm...[a big pause follows] ...57...Q...It seems to have gone out of my
head... I'm sorry.

James: There's no need to be sorry Jemma. This is exactly what is meant to
happen. This is how the mind works. We just gave your internal whiteboard an
impossible task. Hardly anyone can recall over 9 randomly presented units of
information unless they use specialised memory techniques, and I just gave you
10. The whiteboard of our conscious mind really is quite small in size.

## Your mental whiteboard

I'll just explain how the whiteboard process works a little more now. A benefit
of the whiteboard's disappearing ink process is that it is constantly available for
continuous use. As a result of this, huge amounts of information can be written
on the whiteboard during the period of its lifetime. In many respects, it could
be suggested that we should feel grateful that the whiteboard loses access to
information so quickly. If it didn't, it would quite quickly become jammed up
with too much information and it would become unusable.

Taking this idea further, I'd like us to imagine that our out-of-conscious
processes work a little bit like a building that the whiteboard is housed in. I'll just
explain that out-of-conscious processes are brain functions that we are unaware
of, or mental processes that go on in the back of our minds.

Out-of-conscious processes are like a building because the amount of
brain space required for out-of-conscious thinking is absolutely enormous in
comparison to the amount of the brain that is used for the whiteboard. The
building is three-dimensional unlike the two-dimensional whiteboard, and
there are also multiple rooms and secret passageways.

I am using an analogy of a three-dimensional building to represent an idea
that the out-of-conscious mind can think on several different levels at the same
time. It can absorb information from our environment, take care of all of our
bodily functions, plan our activities, assist our communication, and think about
problems we have in our lives without us being consciously aware of it. It can
also use symbols, images, and words to create ideas and connect them up in
a way that we would struggle to do consciously. What it can do is really quite
incredible!

In this building there are filing cabinets crammed with information that we
thought we had forgotten about, and there are reams of papers around waiting
to be filed.

The reams of paper represent thoughts, images and experiences that we have
not fully processed or problems and ideas that we are currently working on.
Many people may have several hundred or even thousands of different thought
strands they are working on at any one time. Thought strands may be about

relationships with different people, hobbies or interests, finances, work projects, holidays, and so forth.

Information does not disappear easily from this building but very often it can get lost or misfiled.

There is so much information in this building or in people's minds that sometimes it is hard for them to find what they are looking for. The more information that's in the building, the harder it is to find what they need. Now imagine that in this building there is a librarian who is very loyal to you and will try to find answers to anything that you ask using the whiteboard, even if it means working through the night. Sometimes the librarian finds information quickly, sometimes it might take days, but when the librarian finds answers to questions posed on the whiteboard it will post an answer on the whiteboard just as soon as there's space.

---

## How does this work in real life?

Let's imagine that you're walking down the street one day and on the other side of the street there is a person whose face you recognise. You are immediately aware that you know this person, but this is not where you normally see him/her. You ask yourself, 'Where do I know him/her from?' a few times. Nothing comes to your mind immediately, and you carry on doing whatever you were doing before. You may even forget that you asked that question as it disappears from your conscious awareness and is replaced by other things. However, a little while later, maybe a few hours, days, or sometimes weeks later, an idea pops into your mind telling you where you had previously seen the person you saw in the street.

A useful rule of thumb, therefore, will be to assume that when we ask our mind a question it will continue to work on questions posed to it even though we may have consciously forgotten that we asked the question in the first place.

Usually the librarian will put thoughts or information in a queue to enter conscious awareness, and in this respect, answers to questions you have asked will wait patiently to pop into your mind when there is space available or when the mind is not occupied with something else. This might explain why some of us can have so many thoughts going through our minds just as we want to go to sleep.

Now ask yourself, what will the librarian come up with if you ask -

'What's wrong with me?', 'Why does this always happen to me?' and, 'Why don't things ever work out for me?'

What will happen if you ask these questions perhaps dozens or even hundreds of times?

It would be great if the librarian could turn around and say, 'You know something, I'm not going to answer these questions. If I go through with what you're asking me to do, I'll just find negative information about you. I'll access your worst memories, filter out any positive bits, ignore your good memories, and give you information that will just make you feel incredibly miserable about yourself. When you feel this way you will ask me to find even more negative information about you, and I'll spend most of my time searching for this negative self-information, rather than doing all of the other fantastic stuff I could be doing. If only you'd just ask me, I could give you information that you could use to change your life.'

But, the librarian can't do that. It is a command-based process. Like an internet search engine it will just recover information that you ask it for, not what you really need, and unfortunately a lot of the time the quality of the information will be innacurate, unchecked and dubious in quality.

## Intrusive thoughts

Common triggers for rumination and worry are intrusive thoughts. Intrusive thoughts tend to contain frightening images or ideas and simply barge their way into awareness whenever they feel like it. The content of intrusive thoughts can be quite threatening in nature and may centre around specific themes, such as losing your: job, partner, friends, life, and your liberty. Intrusive thoughts don't wait around patiently until you're not busy like other thoughts do. They can pop into your mind while you're having a conversation with someone, working, watching TV, or travelling. They're usually accompanied with quite intense emotion, mainly anxiety or guilt.

# Advice from the Black Dog

Rumination generates a mental search process that uses up large amounts of mental energy. It is best to avoid it at all costs.

Intrusive thoughts feel real but they are often less factual than other thoughts.

Negative intrusive thoughts and images, when 'believed' induce intense distress. Awareness of this type of thinking activity will help you to step out of ruminative thinking. Negative, ruminative thinking is so judgemental, critical and crushing. Any time you spend learning about rumination will be invaluable to your recovery and healing.

## CHAPTER 20

# Behavioural experiments

Behavioural experiments can be very important in making changes to your life. The general idea behind them is to teach the self to learn new positive behaviour while breaking patterns of old maladaptive behaviour. To carry out a behavioural experiment, you will need to make a decision to change a behaviour and then put yourself directly in a position to make that behaviour change happen. You will need to make a prediction before you carry out your new behaviour: what you think or feel might happen. When you carry out your new behaviour it is important that you record the results. The majority of us make assumptions about a) how others might react to our behaviour, or b) how we might feel if we carry out a particular behaviour. A lot of the time, however, our assumptions are based on inaccurate information or a lack of knowledge. Behavioural experiments help with the development of experiential knowledge. Experiential knowledge is knowledge that can only be developed through personal experience. Experiential knowledge cannot be learned by thinking about issues or by reading a book. It's something like the difference between reading a book on Africa and actually going to Africa or reading a book about learning to swim and actually swimming. Completing a

behavioural experiment will involve you making a prediction about what you think may occur if you change your behaviour in a particular situation.

After you have made a prediction, you then carry out your new behaviour and observe what occurs. I have made a list of some typical safety behaviours that need be dropped. These types of behaviours are often carried out by people who are in the company of the Black Dog, (see examples below). Most of these behaviours can be challenged using behavioural experiments.

---

### Examples of safety behaviour during depression:

- Say 'Yes' to all requests
- Look for approval from others
- Compare self with others
- Withdraw emotionally
- Hide feelings
- Keep conversations short
- Turn down invitations
- Avoid confrontation
- Use drugs or alcohol to cope
- Ignore feelings
- Drop activities if not feeling 100%

'You won't find out what actually happens
unless you come out of the wardrobe!'

Table 19. Behavioural experiment sheet

**Describe old behaviour or safety behaviour**

Hide true feelings from others

**Describe new behaviour**

Share feelings with a trusted person (Michael).

**How will you carry out new behaviour?**

I am meeting Michael a good friend from work later. I am going to let him know that I have not been feeling myself just lately.

**Predictions about what will happen when you drop the safety behaviour. Write down as many scenarios as possible.**

The conversation might dry up.
Michael might not know what to say and feel awkward.
Our meeting will be for shorter than normal.

**Carry out new behaviour and write down what actually happened here.**

It was difficult, but once I told him it was really helpful. Michael told me that he had similar problems himself in the past. I was completely unaware that he had similar problems. We had quite a long conversation. Michael said that he would be there to talk with me if I needed to. It was just the complete opposite of what I expected.

**What did you learn from this process?**
**How likely are you to carry out this new behaviour again?**

I am really glad I did it. I don't feel so alone. I would do it again, but I'd need to have a think about who I'd feel comfortable enough to speak with.

## Behavioural experiment sheet

**Describe old behaviour or safety behaviour**

**Describe new behaviour**

**How will you carry out new behaviour?**

**Predictions about what will happen when you drop the safety behaviour. Write down as many scenarios as possible.**

**Carry out new behaviour and write down what actually happened here.**

**What did you learn from this process?**
**How likely are you to carry out this new behaviour again?**

# Advice from the Black Dog

Changing your behaviour can make a huge difference to your mood. It is hard to emphasise just how important it is to behave or act differently and how much impact this can have on our wellbeing.

There will always be a time in our life when we need to dig deep and trust our inner courage and bravery.

Take a leap of faith and just see what doing things differently can give you.

## CHAPTER 21

# Using desensitisation

Desensitising means approaching a problem gradually in order to teach the body how to become less affected by it. It is not unlike being inoculated against a disease. When you are inoculated small amounts of a virus or bacteria (generally inactive) are injected into your bloodstream or swallowed by you to teach your body how to cope with more serious strains of a virus or bacteria that you could be exposed to later on. Similarly, desensitisation could also be thought of as behavioural inoculation. Dealing with very mild challenges initially, will help your mind and body cope with more complex challenges later on.

To begin desensitisation, you will need to bring into your awareness all of the safety behaviours that you currently fear dropping and think of all of the things that you have been avoiding. You could complete your list with a trusted person if this helps.

You can start breaking down safety behaviours by following the recipe below. This process can be a little complex so you may need to read through this chapter quite a few times to make it more understandable.

## Recipe for success

Select a potential situation that produces relatively low levels of distress. For example, Vera in our earlier chapter could ask to work in the village shop at a time when there are very few customers.

- List all of the safety behaviours that you generally use in this type of situation. If you need help with this look at the example list of safety behaviours I wrote about earlier.

- Rate every item on your list out of a maximum of 10, in terms of how distressed it might make you feel if you were to drop this safety behaviour or replace it with an alternative behaviour.

- Start by dropping a safety behaviour that produces the lowest level of distress first and follow the procedure below. You will need to repeat the procedure repeatedly until your anxiety drops.

- For each safety behaviour that you want to drop, describe what your new behaviour will be and how you will achieve it. Please see previous chapter .

- Make a prediction about what you think might happen when you carry out an alternative behaviour. Write your prediction down.

- Drop your safety behaviour. (Sometimes safety behaviours are easier to drop if they are replaced with other healthier behaviours.)

- After you have dropped your safety behaviour write down what actually happened when you carried out your alternative behaviour.

- Think about what you learned from the process.

- Pick another safety behaviour with the next lowest level of associated distress, and begin the process again.

## Reducing safety behaviours

One of the best ways to reduce your reliance on safety behaviours is to challenge yourself by collecting evidence about what happens when you drop them. A good way to achieve this is to complete behavioural experiments under different situations. If you are in therapy you can ask your therapist to work with you on dropping particular safety behaviours.

As I mentioned earlier, once you become familiar with dropping the safety behaviours that are the easiest to drop, you can then start dropping behaviours that produce slightly higher levels of discomfort. Whenever you try new approaches, it is very important that you accept your feelings while doing it, as this generally improves the desensitisation process. You will also need to be mindful that when you complete items on your list, that you do so without using any additional safety behaviours, such as holding your breath, distracting yourself, using headphones, and so forth. You will also need to remember that it is not a good idea to move onto more challenging behaviours until your fear about completing less challenging behaviours has reduced significantly or, alternatively, is very easy to tolerate.

Once you have practised dropping your safety behaviours in situations where you have lower anxiety you can then progress through the more difficult types of situations that you might generally avoid. For example, Vera could make things more challenging for herself by asking if she could work during a busy period at the shop.

---

## Using systematic desensitisation in your life

To complete systematic desensitisation you can use the tables on the following pages to write down a list of a) the things that you have been avoiding and b) behaviours that you fear carrying out. Look at each item on your list and rate each item in terms of how much fear each item creates.

To complete a systematic desensitisation process you will need to start working with the least distressing provoking item. Once you have selected something to challenge, read the next chapter titled 'Eposure'. Using the exposure worksheet provided, adopt the new behaviour until your fear is reduced to zero, or until your fear stabilises, and you can easily tolerate your feelings of distress. I'll just mention once more – it is important when you are carrying out systematic desensitisation that you do not move onto exposing yourself to items that evoke higher anxiety until you can easily tolerate lower anxiety evoking items. It is highly beneficial and good practice to repeat behaviours even when they feel mundane and/or boring. I have included the most commonly used sheet on the next page, (see Table 20). Each item on your list can be broken down further, using additional systematic desensitisation sheets.

Table 20. Example of a systematic desensitisation sheet

## Systematic desensitisation sheet

### Overall target situation, object or behaviour for desensitisation

Saying 'No' to requests when I don't really want to do something. I have a 'good friend' and I seem to say 'Yes' to anything she asks and she has taken advantage of that over the years. I don't know how to change things. I feel oppressed by her and her family, but don't want to fall out with them.

| Individual area for desensitisation | Predicted distress level 0 to 10 |
|---|---|
| Say no to sales people that telephone me uninvited. | 1 |
| Tell a sales assistant face to face that I do not need insurance on my electrical appliance. | 3 |
| Tell my 16-year-old daughter that she will need to save up half the money for her school skiing trip. | 4 |
| Explain to customers that I will not be able to see them this week as I am fully booked. | 6 |
| Tell a friend that I am not able to pick up her son from a sports club. | 7 |
| Explain to a friend that her daughter will not be able to stay over at our house during weekdays. | 7 |
| Explain to good friend that I would like her to call me or text me before she turns up at my house uninvited. | 9 |
| Tell good friend that my house will not be available to use as a base on Thursdays going forwards. | 10 |

## Systematic desensitisation sheet

| Overall target situation, object or behaviour for desensitisation | |
| --- | --- |
| **Individual area for desensitisation** | **Predicted distress level 0 to 10** |
| | |
| | |
| | |
| | |
| | |
| | |
| | |
| | |

# Advice from the Black Dog

When you are doing something that you have never done before, you will be more likely to succeed if you concentrate on making small steps, rather than giant leaps. It is remarkable how the tiniest steps in a new direction of our choosing can start to fill us with some hope and confidence in ourselves.

It's true that from tiny acorns great oak trees grow, just as it's true that from positive ideas come positive actions and positive lives.

## CHAPTER 22

# Exposure

Exposure is often used with desensitisation. It involves picking an anxiety evoking behaviour or situation and a) staying in that particular situation or b) continuing to use a particular behaviour until the situation or behaviour is very easy to tolerate. To help yourself reduce your fear in the longer term, assess your anxiety level before, during, and after the situation you have placed yourself in, or while you are using a new behaviour, (see Table 21). After you have completed your exposure work, think about what you have learnt from your experience. This will further embed your experiential learning: learning by doing/experiencing.

Completing behavioural experiments, exposure, and desensitisation can be very difficult, and many people find it easier to work through their lists with the help of a therapist. Most people find that their distress increases significantly when they challenge old ways of thinking and behaving. There does not need to be a timescale for dropping safety behaviours, but if you share what you are attempting to do with a trusted person this can lead to reduced avoidance.

Exposure works well for many people, but not everyone. If you find that your anxiety does not reduce I would suggest that you don't carry on with this approach. It might be the case that you have unprocessed memories that need working through. Unprocessed memories or traumas are events from the past that have not been fully dealt with. They can often be additional factors that create anticipatory fear within the present time mode. Once unprocessed memories are worked through, which generally requires a therapist, it will then be a lot easier to drop safety behaviours at a later stage.

Table 21. Example of an exposure sheet

| Time:<br>Date: | Situation | Anxiety before (0 to 10 where 10 is max) | Anxiety during (0 to 10 where 10 is max) | Anxiety after (0 to 10 where 10 is max) | What did I learn? |
|---|---|---|---|---|---|
| | | | | | |

# Advice from the Black Dog

Exposure can be very difficult initially as it can leave you feeling very uncomfortable. Stay with your feelings and most of the time they will gradually fade away.

Finding out 'in this moment' that we are not in danger or under threat is extremely beneficial in both the short-and long-term. We can think of exposure work as if we were grasping a nettle. Once embraced there is no further shock of pain and the pain gradually subsides.

## CHAPTER 23

# Help with the Black Dog

A s I mentioned in previous chapters, there are likely to be hundreds of different factors that can influence depression, from diet and daylight hours to relationships with others. If anyone claims a cure all for depression, or if an author says that a book can cure depression just by reading it, in my opinion they are likely to be a charlatan. CBT strategies tend to reduce symptoms of depression, but the research evidence indicates that in most cases CBT does not eliminate the symptoms entirely.

## Medication

Medication is still the most commonly used treatment for depression and evidence indicates that a combination of CBT and medication is more beneficial than using either approach alone. There are logical reasons that explain why medication enhances a CBT approach. If, at an organic level, the mind does not have the capacity to think straight there is very little likelihood that people will have the concentration or energy to complete CBT exercises effectively, or to make any of the changes I have covered in this book. Medication may give people the extra energy or boost required to make these changes. Equally, if you take medication without making any changes to your behaviour you will not be making the best use of your medication. SSRI medication does not add extra brain serotonin, it simply helps you to utilise the serotonin that you already have more effectively.

Some people who become depressed start to withdraw from activities and social events that they previously enjoyed, which can lead to self-perpetuating symptoms of depression. Medication can help people to lift themselves out of a depressed position, and when this happens they once again feel able to resume normal activities, lift themselves up, and maintain a positive mood state. In this respect, medication can be viewed as a pick-me-up that helps people carry on down their path once more. Medication does not, however, resolve the issue of what initially makes people become depressed.

## Mindfulness

Growing evidence indicates that mindfulness can be very helpful for people who experience repeated episodes of depression. In my experience it tends to work because it:

- Encourages the processing and observation of feelings.

- Helps people to stay in the present moment and detach themselves from ruminative thinking.

- Exercises the prefrontal cortex which then becomes more effective at 1) reducing background noise in the mind, and 2) regulating emotions.

Mindfulness also has a large element of compassionate-based thinking, which deters individuals from engaging in interpersonal conflict. (Many individuals with depression are likely to struggle with interpersonal conflict issues due to deficits in their anterior cingulate.)

As with the use of CBT exercises, you will need to keep using mindfulness-based approaches in order to maintain your positive mood state. Being mindful will also help you become much more aware of the types of environment and people that impact on your mood state. With awareness comes choice. You can choose to move away from negative environments and negative people if you wish. Equally, you can choose to think negatively about others or you can choose to think compassionately.

A mindfulness practice can be incorporated into many daily activities to make good use of your time. You can practise mindfulness in the shower, while eating, running, driving, and doing housework. The list is endless really. Practising mindfulness does not necessarily need additional time once you have taken the time to learn how to complete the exercises.

## Parks Inner Child Therapy

One of the most effective therapies that I have come across for de-stabilising maladaptive beliefs is Parks Inner Child Therapy or PICT. For some people their belief systems are so rigid and entrenched that CBT is not powerful enough on its own to create flexibility in belief systems. Developed by Penny Parks, a survivor of sexual abuse, PICT works quickly to change belief patterns, which in turn helps to make rules more flexible. PICT exercises have the power to reduce the impact of a) vicarious trauma and b) unhelpful maladaptive processes learnt from parents. Changes appear to occur mainly out of conscious awareness. PICT has yet to be researched fully at an empirical level, although small-scale scientific studies have found that it has a very powerful effect on depressed individuals.

I had my own PICT therapy, and I completed a year's training in it to reach diploma level. I found that the exercises had the ability to facilitate rapid personal change. After completing PICT exercises my beliefs did not seem as believable as before, and it was a lot easier to stand back from my beliefs and to change my behaviour. PICT is quite dependent on therapeutic input, and although PICT trainers recommend using PICT exercises on your own, in practice it is very difficult due to the high levels of concentration required. This is one of the major drawbacks of PICT. When I have offered PICT by itself to clients I have found that it does not have the longevity of change associated with therapies such as CBT and Mindfulness, where clients can practise a lot of the exercises on their own. On the other hand, I have also found that when PICT is combined with CBT approaches, belief change can be sustained for far longer periods. I will describe one of the more straightforward exercises from PICT below for you: The future most developed self.

## The future most developed self (FMDS) exercise

The FMDS exercise (see Table 22) is designed to help you focus on the person that you intend to become someday. It is a self in the future, a person you will become when you have made all of the changes that you feel you need to make. It is a person who chooses how he or she lives his/her daily life. This self has all of the necessary inner resources (e.g., compassion, kindness etc.) and coping strategies to make the most of life.

The best place to start when using this exercise is to select a problem that you have experienced recently. This will be a problem involving at least one other person. It will be a problem that you feel you have not handled very well, and even now when you think about it, you will be unsure how you could have handled things differently. Run that problem through in your mind and assess how you dealt with it and think about how you felt afterwards.

To complete the exercise do whatever you need to do to keep the image of your FMDS in mind. Think about the way he/she looks, thinks, feels, and behaves. Once you have completed the construction of your FMDS image step inside your FMDS and watch from inside your FMDS as he/she resolves your problem for you on your behalf. Bear in mind that when your FMDS is solving your problem for you, your everyday self (i.e., the self inside your FMDS) will be a passive observer and will not do or say anything. The everyday self will simply be watching, listening and feeling how the FMDS feels and noticing what the FMDS does. Once your FMDS has resolved your problem, step outside of your FMDS and assess how he or she may have reacted to your problem differently.

## Eye Movement Desensitisation & Reprocessing (EMDR)

EMDR is best known for its use with individuals suffering from Post-Traumatic Stress Disorder. Rapid eye movement is used in conjunction with accessing traumas, which allows people to process partially processed or unprocessed memories. As unprocessed memories are stored in subcortical regions of the brain, there is a tendency for many individuals to become emotionally distressed in environments that have cues connected to those previous memories. When this occurs, people can feel emotionally distressed, but will often not understand why.

From my experience of EMDR I was surprised at how effective it was. I went onto the training not understanding how it might work and feeling highly sceptical. I was pleasantly surprised at how quickly the process worked and how effective it was. After working on a number of childhood memories I felt more at ease generally. It was as if my anxiety levels had been turned down a notch or two. I had already worked on the same memories previously using person-centred therapy, psychodynamic therapy, neurolinguistic programming, CBT, and PICT. EMDR had the most powerful effect on these memories, taking away all the painful emotion connected to them. I felt calmer and relaxed afterwards and the effects were sustained permanently for these particular memories.

Table 22. Future most developed self worksheet

## Future most developed self exercise – Sheet 1

**What are the main differences between your future most developed self and the way that you are today?**

He has more grey hair. He has an improved posture. He appears more serene. He appears lighter in weight and looks physically healthy. He appears more spiritually aware.

**What do you notice from what you see that this is the case?**

I can see his grey hair. He holds himself better and looks calm. He looks unruffled as though he is taking the world in his stride. He looks young for his years.

**Describe facial expression**

He has a gentle smile. His brow is relaxed. He has open approachable, compassionate eyes.

**Describe posture and body language**

He holds himself in a mindful way. He has an open posture and is upright.

**Describe hairstyle, physical appearance, clothing, footwear, makeup and jewellery etc**

He is wearing loose-fitting natural fabrics. Light grey with possibly an Eastern feeling.

**How does your 'future most developed self' sound when speaking?**

He sounds calm and relaxed. He listens more than he speaks. He is softly spoken and gentle.

**How does your 'future most developed self feel? Where in his/her body are these feelings experienced?**

Calm and relaxed. He feels as though he is touch with the Universe. He feels these feelings in his chest, his arms, his legs, and his stomach.

## Future most developed self exercise – Sheet 2

**What do you notice about the way that your 'future most developed self' interacts with others?**

Patient and kind. He uses thoughtful questions. He can still regress to his childhood with his friends. He is polite and he can be gregarious when he needs to be.

**What does your 'future most developed self' believe about him/herself?**

He has nothing to prove but he knows he can add a lot and he wants to do this. He knows that he has come a long way in his life and he lives his life with daily gratitude for that. He recognises how fortunate he is.

**If your 'future most developed self' was asked what has led to her/him becoming the person that she/he currently is, what would he/she say?**

Choose to spend more time in each moment. Approach each small moment with gratitude and love. Enjoy the experience of life and embrace the human experience.

**Step inside your 'future most developed self.' How does it feel to be in her/his body?**

Calm and connected with the Universe. Energy buzzing through the body.

**Watch from beginning to end as your 'future most developed self' resolves a difficulty for you on your behalf.**

**What did you learn from your 'future most developed self?**

He approaches helping others close to him in a kinaesthetic/healing way.

What do you make of the fact that the way that your 'future most developed self' resolved your problem all came from within you?

It's quite incredible. I feel as though I am evolving towards the person that I already am and letting go of the damage of previous generations.

## Future most developed self exercise – Sheet 1

What are the main differences between your future most developed self and the way that you are today?

What do you notice from what you see that this is the case?

Describe facial expression

Describe posture and body language

Describe hairstyle, physical appearance, clothing, footwear, makeup and jewellery etc

How does your 'future most developed self' sound when speaking?

How does your 'future most developed self' feel? Where in his/her body are these feelings experienced?

## Future most developed self exercise – Sheet 2

What do you notice about the way that your 'future most developed self' interacts with others?

What does your 'future most developed self' believe about him/herself?

If your 'future most developed self' was asked what has led to her/him becoming the person that she/he currently is, what would he/she say?

Step inside your 'future most developed self.' How does it feel to be in her/his body?

Watch from beginning to end as your 'future most developed self' resolves a difficulty for you on your behalf.

What did you learn from your 'future most developed self?

What do you make of the fact that the way that your 'future most developed self' resolved your problem all came from within you?

# Advice from the Black Dog

A combination of both CBT and medication can work very effectively for depression. Mindfulness can be useful to detach yourself from worrying and rumination. EMDR can help to reduce symptoms that result from traumatic experiences.

There are a range of interventions and strategies that can help support our wellbeing. Which ever intervention you are using, central to all therapeutic approaches is curiosity, patience, kindness, forgiveness where necessary, and the love of your own vulnerability. It is also important to remember the simultaneously fragile yet magnificent creature that you are.

## CHAPTER 24

# Conclusion

Y ou have now come to the end of this book and hopefully you have a better understanding of your Black Dog. You may also need to be aware that forming an improved relationship with the Black Dog will involve you changing a) the way that you think, b) how you relate to your feelings, and c) how you behave. Changing the way that you think, feel, and behave is not as easy as it might seem, even if change is considered a good thing.

You are highly likely to meet resistance from yourself when you begin to approach change. But when you can get past this resistance, you may learn new things from your new experiences, and you can use what you learn for the future – hopefully, even for the rest of your life. As humans, we have an inbuilt resistance to change. I'll explain what I mean using an example from science. Let's imagine that in the past a common view was that the world was flat. This fact 'the world is flat, was challenged by one scientist describing an alternative worldview, in this case 'the world is round'. The scientist's new idea was supported by some evidence, for example, the horizon appeared to have a slight curvature. The scientist's new suggestions met resistance from the general population as certainty was replaced by uncertainty, or as the previously stable view of the world was challenged. Suggestions were put forward to test the new theory; for example, someone said, 'Let's organise a sailing expedition!' A man called Magellan volunteered to complete the expedition and he set off to circumnavigate the world. Uncertainty, unrest, resistance and anxiety increased still further, as the challenge to the old worldview became experiential. As I mentioned earlier, experiential means that we are experiencing things directly for ourselves rather than simply thinking about them logically. The experiential phase of change is the most anxiety provoking for humans as it presents a position of not knowing. Potentially it is also one of the most frightening positions a thinking, or conceptualising animal can find him or herself in, and hence why we have such a built-in avoidance of it. Not knowing is associated with danger and we are instinctively programmed to avoid what we perceive as dangerous.

Eventually, Magellan came back and the findings of his voyage were inspected, and the results measured. In this case, the crew from Magellan's expedition brought back items from the other side of the world, drew new revised maps, and reported that the world was not flat. The previous view of the world had begun to change. For a while there was still resistance. People disbelieved the evidence even though it was staring them in the face, and it was difficult for them to dispute it. However, after a period of time, uncertainty was gradually replaced by certainty and confidence in the new idea was reinforced. People's anxiety reduced and a period of reflection on the outcome followed. Eventually, the new worldview was adopted by enough people, and it then became viewed as a fact. After a while the whole process started again, when another scientist suggested that the world was not round it was a sphere flattened at its poles.

I am suggesting that your journey will follow a pattern in a predetermined order. A period of uncertainty will take place before change occurs. In this respect, as you approach the strategies that you will come across in this book, periods of experiential uncertainty will become a natural and arguably essential part of your learning process. If you decide to embrace your uncertainty about completing new exercises or new coping strategies, you will find that your uncertainty like a chrysalis will be used to transform you. Your period of uncertainty will pass and you will emerge from your old shell with increased confidence. Your distress will reduce and you will begin to reflect on the outcomes that you have achieved. The process will then begin again with the next new exercise that you try.

If you notice that you want to resist change, this is completely natural. In my years as a clinical psychologist, fear of change has cropped up frequently in my professional life. Embarrassingly, I will admit to you now that I initially resist learning new therapeutic approaches, thinking my current approach is the best and only way. I then approach the new area of therapy and feel fear, anxiety, and uncertainty while I learn to practice it. You see, at this point new approaches represent a challenge to my previous view – what I thought I knew – and I feel generally incompetent. I then gain the necessary knowledge to use the new approach, and my confidence in using it increases. The process then starts over again the next time I come across something new. Each time I do this I learn new things that can complement and improve my understanding.

Another area that you will need to confront is habitual behaviour. Much of the time we can find ourselves falling into repetitive loops or habitual behaviours when we become highly emotional. (Habitual behaviours are behaviours that occur automatically.) Many of us use the same habitual behaviours over and over again to deal with our emotions in certain situations, even when we know that our strategies don't work. As I mentioned earlier, traditional neuroscience suggests that the foundation of habit formation can be found in the basal ganglia, a subcortical region of the brain. When we become distressed, states of high emotional arousal lead to primitive brain areas, located in the subcortical area, taking a central role. These primitive brain areas are governed by habitual behaviour, which tends to be automatic, inflexible and rule based. Habitual behaviour is generally thought to operate outside of conscious awareness and we revert to this quite strongly when under stress or when we are tired.

Very best of luck with your Black Dog

# Regulatory organisations in the UK

British Association of Cognitive and Behavioural Psychotherapists
Imperial House
Hornby Street
Bury
Lancashire
BL9 5BN
Tel: 0161 705 4304   Fax: 0161 705 4306
Email: babcp@babcp.com

British Association for Counselling & Psychotherapy
BACP House
15 St John's Business Park
Lutterworth
LE17 4HB
Tel 01455 883300

British Psychological Society
St Andrews House
48 Princess Road East
Leicester
LE1 7DR
United Kingdom
Tel: +44 (0)116 254 9568
Fax: +44 (0)116 227 1314
Email: enquiries@bps.org.uk

Health & Care Professional Council
Park House
184 Kennington Park Road,
London, SE11 4BU
0300 500 6184

# References and additional reading

Arnsten, A., Raskind, M., Taylor, F. & Connor, D. (2015) The effects of stress exposure on prefrontal cortex: Translating basic research into successful treatments for post-traumatic stress disorder. Neurobiology of Stress, pp. 89–99.

Bandura, A. (1977) Social Learning Theory. Prentice-Hall.

Beck, J. (2011) Cognitive Behavior Therapy: Second Edition – Basics and Beyond. The Guildford Press.

Butler, G. (2009). Overcoming Social Anxiety & Shyness. Robinson

Cabral, R. & Nardi E. (2012) Anxiety and inhibition of panic attacks within translational and prospective research contexts. Trends in Psychiatry.

Clark, D.M. (1986) A cognitive approach to panic. Behaviour Research and Therapy, 24: 461–470.

Clark, D.M. & Wells, A. (1995) A cognitive model of social phobia. In Social Phobia – Diagnosis, Assessment, and Treatment (eds. R.G. Heimberg, M.R. Liebowitz, D. Hope et al.), pp. 69–93. New York: Guilford.

Debiec, J. & Sullivan, R. (2014) Intergenerational transmission of emotional trauma through amygdala-dependent mother-to-infant transfer of specific fear. Proceedings of the National Academy of Sciences, DOI: 10.1073/pnas.1316740111

Golman, D. (1996) Emotional Intelligence: Why It Can Matter More Than IQ. Bloomsbury.

Greenberger, D. & Padesky, C. (1995) Mind Over Mood: Change How You Feel by Changing the Way That You Think. Guildford Press.

Guzmán, Y., Tronson, N., Jovasevic, K., Sato, K., Guedea, A., Mizukami, H., Nishimori, K. & Radulovic. J. (2013) Fear-enhancing effects of septal oxytocin receptors. Nature Neuroscience, DOI: 10.1038/nn.3465.

Kennerley, H. (2009) Overcoming Anxiety: A Self-Help Guide Using Cognitive Behavioural Techniques. Robinson.

Kinman, G. & Grant, L. (2010) Exploring stress resilience in trainee social workers: The role of emotional and social competencies. British Journal of Social Work, 10.1093/bjsw/bcq088.

Krusemark, E. & Li, W. (2012) Enhanced olfactory sensory perception of threat in anxiety: An event-related fMRI study. Chemosensory Perception, 5(1): 37 DOI: 10.1007/s12078-011-9111-7.

LeDoux, J.E., Iwata, J., Cicchetti, P., Reis, D.J. (1988) Different projections of the central amygdaloid nucleus mediate autonomic and behavioral correlates of conditioned fear. Journal of Neuroscience, Jul;8(7): 2517–29.

Logue, M.W., Bauver, S.R., Kremen, W.S., Franz, C.E., Eisen, S.A., Tsuang, M.T., Grant, M.D. & Lyons, M.J. (2011) Evidence of overlapping genetic diathesis of panic attacks and gastrointestinal disorders in a sample of male twin pairs. Twin Research and Human Genetics, Feb; 14(1): 16–24. doi: 10.1375/twin.14.1.16.

Moorey, S. (2010) The six cycles maintenance model: Growing a 'vicious flower' for depression. Behaviour and Cognitive Psychotherapy, Mar; 38(2): 173–84. Moulding, R., Coles, M.E., Abramowitz, J.S., Alcolado, G.M., Alonso, P., Belloch, A., Bouvard, M., Clark, D.A., Doron, G., Fernández-Álvarez, H., García-Soriano, G., Ghisi, M., Gómez, B., Inozu, M., Radomsky, A.S., Shams, G., Sica, C., Simos, G. & Wong, W. (2014) Part 2. They scare because we care: the relationship between obsessive intrusive thoughts and appraisals and control strategies across 15 cities. Journal of Obsessive-Compulsive and Related Disorders, 3(3): 280–291.

Rachman, S., Coughtrey, S.R. & Radomsky, A. (2015) The Oxford Guide to the Treatment of Mental Contamination. The Oxford University Press.

Seger, C.A. (2011) A critical review of habit learning and the basal ganglia. Frontiers in Systems Neuroscience, Aug 30; 5:66.

Teachman, B., Marker, C. & Clerkin, E. (2010) Catastrophic misinterpretations as a predictor of symptom change during treatment for panic disorder. Journal of Consulting and Clinical Psychology, 78(6): 964–973.

Veale, D. & Wilson, R. (2005) Overcoming Obsessive Compulsive Disorder: A Self-help Guide using Cognitive Behavioral Techniques. ConsTable & Robinson Ltd.

Wells, A. (1997) Cognitive Therapy of Anxiety Disorders: A Practice Manual and Conceptual Guide. Wiley.

Wilson, R. & Veale, D. (2009) Overcoming Health Anxiety. Robinson.

# Glossary

Academics: Academics spend a lot of time studying or researching specialist subjects at institutions like universities.

Abdominal breathing: Processing of breathing which involves relaxing the abdomen and taking in air to the bottom of the lungs.

Amygdala: Small area of brain tissue within the limbic system, responsible for activating the body's fight-flight-or-freeze response.

Anxiety: An emotion which is experienced when the body is moving into a prepared state to deal with a potential threat.

Automatic responses: Responses which occur automatically/outside of conscious awareness.

Behavioural strategies: Making an adjustment to your behaviour and monitoring the impact of resulting changes.

Catastrophic misinterpretation: A frightening and exaggerated thought connected to magnification of perceived stimuli.

Catecholamines: Chemical messengers used by cells to communicate with one and other.

Cognitive distortions: Thinking patterns that distort perception of reality.

Cognitive interventions: Strategies based on changing mental reactions.

Conditioned response: A response that occurs automatically as a result of repeated actions towards particular stimuli.

Coping strategies: Strategies that have been of some assistance in reducing distress.

Core beliefs: Strongly held beliefs about the self.

Counter-intuitive: Ideas which we would not naturally gravitate towards.

Default response: An automatic response based on previous experiences and past conditioning.

Desensitising: Gradually being able to tolerate a feeling by staying in a situation until the feeling feels more bearable.

Diazepam: A medication often prescribed as a muscle relaxant.

Dissociation: A mental and physical state where an individual feels a loss of connection with his or her body.

Distraction: A process that individuals use to avoid experiencing painful emotions.

Emotional reference point: A mechanism used by babies who look towards caregivers to determine how they might react at an emotional level.

Experiential: A process of experiencing through the senses.

External focus: Placing one's attention onto one's external environment.

Habitual behaviours: Behaviours that we are inclined to use because we have used them so many times before.

Hyperventilation: A process of rapid shallow breathing where an individual breathes out too much carbon dioxide.

Hypothesis: An idea based on scientific theory.

Intrusive thoughts: Thoughts that enter awareness uninvited. These thoughts are usually accompanied by heightened emotion.

Mindfulness: A process of staying in the present moment, bringing conscious awareness back to the present, and deliberately moving away from thoughts about the past or the future.

Mood regulation: An ability to have some management of one's feelings.

Negative automatic thoughts: Thoughts in the background of the mind that have the potential to keep individuals emotionally distressed.

Negative reinforcement: A process of repeated behaviour in which negative emotion is reduced leading to greater likelihood of the same future behaviour.

Neocortex: Highly developed area of the mind responsible for logical, rational and analytical thinking.

Phobic response: An automatic response associated with heightened anxiety, connected to a specific trigger or cue.

Plasticity: The brains ability to repair itself and grow the more that it is used.

Prefrontal cortex: An area of the brain that acts as a relay between the subcortical regions of the brain and the neocortex. It is also responsible for dampening emotional reactions and quietening the mind.

Registered therapists: Registered therapists are members of professional bodies. Professional bodies are organisations that check out their therapists to make sure that they have the required training to do their jobs properly.

Rumination: A cognitive process which involves churning of thoughts connected to the self in the past over and over in the mind.

Safety behaviours: Behaviours utilised to reduce emotional distress in the short-term.

Self-fulfilling prophecy: When something occurs despite your very best attempts to prevent that particular thing occurring.

Self-perpetuating: A situation that is kept in place through its own actions.

Subcortical regions: Brain areas located in the lower half of the brain.

Suppressing emotions: An act of pushing down painful or upsetting feelings.

Threat Perception Centre: An area within the brain responsible to noticing stimuli associated with past fear or trauma.

Traumatic incidents: Events that have occurred in the past connected to highly distressing emotions.

# Common Medications

Alprazolam: A benzodiazepine prescribed for panic, generalised anxiety, phobias, social anxiety, OCD

Amitriptyline: A tricyclic antidepressant

Atenolol: A beta-blocker prescribed for anxiety

Buspirone: A mild tranquiliser prescribed for generalised anxiety, OCD and panic

Chlordiazepoxide: A benzodiazepine prescribed for generalised anxiety, phobias

Citalopram: A selective serotonin reuptake inhibitor commonly prescribed for mixed anxiety and depression

Clomipramine: A tricyclic antidepressant

Clonazepam: A benzodiazepine prescribed for panic, generalised anxiety, phobias, social anxiety

Desipramine: A tricyclic anti-depressant

Diazepam: A benzodiazepine prescribed for generalised anxiety, panic, phobias

Doxepin: A tricyclic antidepressant

Duloxetine: A serotonin-norepinephrine reuptake inhibitor

Escitalopram Oxalate: A selective serotonin reuptake inhibitor

Fluoxetine: A selective serotonin reuptake inhibitor

Fluvoxamine: A selective serotonin reuptake inhibitor

Gabapentin: An anticonvulsant prescribed for generalised anxiety and social anxiety

Imipramine: A tri-cyclic antidepressant

Lorazepam: A benzodiazepine prescribed for generalised anxiety, panic, phobias

Nortriptyline: A tricyclic antidepressant

Oxazepam: A benzodiazepine prescribed for generalised anxiety, phobias

Paroxetine: A selective serotonin reuptake inhibitor

Phenelzine: A monoamine oxidase inhibitor

Pregabalin: An anticonvulsant prescribed for generalised anxiety disorder

Propanalol: A beta blocker prescribed for anxiety

Sertraline: A selective serotonin reuptake inhibitor

Tranylcypromine: A monoamine oxidase inhibitor

Valproate: An anti-convulsant prescribed for panic

Venlafaxine: A serotonin-norepinephrine reuptake inhibitor

# Index

Activity schedule,18
Basal ganglia, 131
Behavioural experiments, 104, 115, 135
Behavioural strategies, 132
Beliefs, 65, 70, 75, 79, 89, 92
Cognitive distortions, 44, 132, 135
Cognitive interventions,132
Conscious mind, 99, 100
Cortisol,14, 17
Depression,, 131, 134
Desensitising, 109, 132
Diet,14
DSM-V, 2
Eleanor Maguire, 38
EMDR, 120, 121, 126, 135
Experiential avoidance, 89
Exposure, 112, 115, 117, 130, 135
Future most developed self, 120
Habitual behaviours, 128, 133
Intrusive thoughts, 102, 103, 133, 135
Limiting beliefs, 60
Medication, 118, 119, 135
Mental whiteboard, 100
Mindfulness, 11, 119, 120, 126, 133, 135
Mood diaries,18
NAT challenging, 75, 81, 83, 84
Negative reinforcement, 34, 35, 133, 135
Neocortex, 5, 133, 135

Parks Inner Child Therapy, 119
Prefrontal, 6,, 133, 135
Problem list, 27
Research, 130
Rules, 48, 51, 53, 54, 135
Rumination, 11, 15, 32, 33, 98, 102, 103, 126, 138, 140
Safety behaviours, 34, 60, 65, 90, 92, 105, 109, 110, 115
Self- observation, 37
Serotonin,13, 14
Social learning, 62, 135
SSRIs, 13, 14
Subcortical, 5, 6, 7, 8, 31, 32, 38, 89, 90, 93, 96, 121, 128, 133
Thought diaries, 39
Winston Churchill, 1, 36
Worry, 98, 135

# Advice for loved ones

When I experienced depression I felt blamed and judged by the people close to me and the essence of the feedback I got from close family members was that there was something intrinsically wrong me for feeling the way I did. In short, sympathy was in very limited supply! People who do not have a history of depression, do not know what it's like to be depressed and they tend to know very little about the neurobiology of depression. Depression rarely occurs in isolation and symptoms associated with it are often highly reactive and easily influenced by the behaviours of others. Others can have much more of an impact on depression than either they or we realise. Please share this chapter with loved ones, as there are many things that they can do to help you to move out of a depressed position.

---

### There is a big difference between low mood and depression?

Nearly all of us at some point in our life will experience low mood. Low mood is a normal reaction to loss, set-backs and failures that we all face from time to time. For most of us our low mood passes relatively quickly and causes little disruption.

Depression, on the other hand, is a problem that hangs on for longer periods of time, often causing much more disruption to our lives. Individuals who experience depression have low mood, but are also likely to experience problems with their concentration, memory, sleep, appetite, motivation, energy, libido, and ways of thinking.

---

### Depression is still a widely misunderstood problem.

Ironically, although depression is very common in our society - during our lives at least one in four of us will experience a significant period of depression - it is still clouded by misunderstanding. Depression often does not make sense to those who have never experienced it. This lack of understanding can often leave individuals who experience depression feeling even worse about themselves.

---

### Depression is like a trap from which it's hard to escape.

For those who experience depression, it can feel like a trap in which the more effort that is used trying to escape from it, the more stuck a person tends to feel. It's not dissimilar to falling into quicksand. Struggling doesn't work, and the strategy that is needed to get out (being still) feels counter-intuitive.

**Is positive intention enough?**

Our natural instinct when we see someone we love suffering is to try to help. The way we attempt to help someone with depression is very important, because many behaviours even if carried out with the best intentions can be harmful, contributing to mood deterioration. When this occurs, we can end up feeling just as helpless as our loved one does. If you find yourself identifying with some of the things that I have outlined, it is likely that you may experience some discomfort or even some guilt. If this is your experience, it will be important to remind yourself of three essential ideas.

- Guilt is a powerful motivating force. It influences us to change our behaviour.

- It would be easier for all of us if we could do things in retrospect. Unless we are professionally trained none of us are taught how to help others with depression. We simply do the best that we can.

- Use any painful or uncomfortable feelings you experience as an incentive to make positive changes. Forgive yourself your past mistakes and start afresh from today.

I have outlined eight traps below that many family members and people close to people with depression naturally fall into. I am going to suggest that you look out for these as much as possible and try to avoid them.

# Trap 1. Questioning

## Examples of questioning:

'Why are you feeling like this?'
'What's the matter with you?'
'What's wrong?'

## Positive intention behind questioning

We use questions such as those above, to gather information so that we can help our loved ones feel better.

## Result of questioning on the individual with depression

Individuals who are depressed will have already asked themselves the very same questions over and over again. Asking such questions instigates an internal problem-solving process that simply brings more negative self-opinion and self-judgement into their awareness. Your questions will provide further evidence that there is something wrong with loved one. This creates material for further rumination, which ultimately keeps their low mood in place. Unfortunately, when your loved one is depressed, such questions can also be perceived as judgemental or critical and will discourage dialogue.

## Potential impact on you

Your use of questioning could end up with you feeling helpless and low in respect of your inability to resolve the situation.

## Trap 2. Rationalising

**Example of rationalising**

'You don't need to feel like this!'
'Look at what you have got. You've got a loving family, you've got a nice house."'
'Lots of people would be grateful just to be in your position.'

**Positive intention behind rationalising**

You rationalise because you want to be helpful. You want your loved one to realise that life is much better than he or she thinks, and to recognise that there is no real reason why he/she should feel depressed.

**Result**

Individuals who experience depression are likely to be highly analytical and already know the facts about their situation. The message your loved one will receive is that they are wrong in feeling the way they do. Feeling wrong about their feelings simply contributes further to their feelings of low mood, and fuels ideas that there is something defective about them.

**Potential impact on you**

You may see your loved one attempting to put on a positive front, as he/she attempts to hide his/her feelings, and please you. When this occurs you may end up feeling as though you're speaking to a veneer, without any sense of true connection.

## Trap 3. Providing solutions or advice

### Example of providing solutions or advice

'What you need to do is this...'
'If I were you...'
'If I were you I would...'
'Why don't you...?'
'Have you thought about going to...?'

### Positive intention behind offering solutions and advice

You offer solutions and advice to be helpful. The answers seem so clear, so why can't your loved one see it?

### Result

Your loved one already knows that he or she could do things differently, but when he/she is depressed he/she doesn't know what to do for the best, or how to do it. There's also a high risk of you being perceived as critical and controlling – This will instigate a thinking process whereby your loved one reflects about why he/she hasn't done what you've suggested already. This provides further fuel for cycles of rumination, which keeps his or her low mood in place. Your loved one is also likely to feel misunderstood, further enhancing his/her feelings of failure, isolation and loneliness.

### Potential impact on you

You may end up feeling disempowered and frustrated, for although in your mind you will have offered good advice, you will also have to watch as your advice fails to be followed.

# Trap 4. Disapproving of your loved one's low mood

## Examples of disapproval

Shouting.

Losing your temper.

Using behavioural gestures such as rolling your eyes, or shaking your head.

## Positive intention behind disapproval

When you show disapproval, your intention is to help your loved one understand that depression is bad for them. You think that if we show enough disapproval, then he or she might simply stop feeling the way he or she does or that their depressed mood might simply go away.

## Result

Many individuals who experience depression have learnt (often in their childhood) that their self-worth is conditional on the approval that they get from others. Your behaviour may lead them to try not to be depressed or to try to control their low mood. These types of behaviour can lead to him/her feeling progressively lower. Your loved one may also try to hide his/her low mood from you, leaving him/her feeling even more isolated, embarrassed and ashamed about the way he/she feels.

## Potential impact on you

You are more likely to continue feeling frustrated, and after reflection you may also experience shame and guilt about your own behaviour.

## Trap 5. Avoiding your loved one's low mood

### Examples of avoiding low mood

Spending more time at work, away from your loved one.
Creating reasons why you need to be somewhere else.

### Positive intention behind avoiding low mood

Many times, when you avoid your loved ones low mood you will not even be aware that you are doing it. But sometimes you may avoid him/her consciously because you feel you cannot do anything to change the situation. You may justify to yourself about why it is best to have less contact. Alternatively, you may think that if maybe you spend more time around your loved one when they are low, that you are encouraging their low mood in some way, and if you avoid it, it will go away by itself.

### Result

Individuals who experience depression are likely to personalise your behaviour as meaning something negative about them, and then use this as evidence to support their beliefs of low worth, not being good enough or insignificant etc. From a behavioural point of view they are also likely to be spending more time on their own, feeling lonely.

### Potential impact on you

You may end up feeling that you are drifting further and further apart from your loved one and feel more helpless about resolving the situation.

## Trap 6. Criticising and teaching

### Examples of criticism

'You're weak. …pathetic.'
'Are you going to stay in your room for ever?'
'It's not normal to behave this way!'
'Why don't you just get over it?'
'Don't you realise how you make me feel when you do this?'
'Have you considered the effect your behaviour has on the rest of us?'

### Positive intention behind criticism

When you are critical to our loved ones, you want them to see the error of their ways and to decide to be different and to change their behaviour. You are critical, because you care, and it's normal to be more critical with people who we love the most.

When you attempt to teach, you are trying to be helpful. You want your loved one to understand that his/her symptoms of depression can have an impact on others. Your aim is to help your loved one to take responsibility for the way that he/she is feeling and to help him/her make positive changes for him/herself.

### Result

Your loved one experiencing depression may not realise that your reaction to him/her is driven by our own fear, anxiety, or sense of responsibility for his/her well-being. Individuals who are susceptible to depression already tend to be highly self-critical, and often are far more critical about themselves than you will be. Your criticisms will simply be used to confirm or supply further evidence for the negative thoughts that he/she already had about him/herself.

Your loved one will be more likely to think that he/she is causing harm to others because of the way that he/she feels. Individuals who are susceptible to depression already feel guilty and ashamed when they feel low, and your comments will simply reinforce these feelings. Individuals who experience depression often have a tendency to want to please others, and your comments will reinforce within them the idea that other people's feelings are more important than theirs. Teaching may also send a subtle message to your loved one that his/her feelings are unbearable, unacceptable, or faulty in some way.

### Potential impact on you

Your criticisms are unlikely to improve the situation for our loved ones. As well as this you may end up feeling powerless, ashamed, frustrated and guilty. You will also have to watch as he/she becomes angry or even more withdrawn.

## Trap 7. Overprotection

### Examples of over-protection

Helping our loved one to avoid feeling upset by taking over tasks that they would normally carry out. Telling others how to behave towards them, for example; 'Don't upset your mother, brother, father', 'Watch what you're saying please.'

### Positive intention behind overprotection.

To protect your loved one from potential further low mood

### Result

When you over-protect, you demonstrate to your loved one, that you think that he/she is not capable of looking after him/herself. This is likely to exacerbate his/her feelings of low self-worth, and increase his/her avoidance, which will contribute to him/her experiencing continued depression. His/her problems will seem even more significant if he/she perceives that you are helping him/her to avoid things. Over protection is also likely to project feelings of fragility and helplessness in your loved one.

### Potential impact on you

You may end up feeling increasingly anxious as your attempts to protect your loved one result in little improvement. Confusion and resentment may also set in, as the more you are doing to "help" your loved one the more disabled and withdrawn he/she appears to become.

## You can make a big difference

The fact that you are reading this chapter shows that you already have high levels of positive intention. So let's turn this intention into results that work. Read the ideas covered in the next few pages and understand them. Discussing them with your loved one will also be helpful.

### Fighting low mood does not work!

The process of fighting depression is not unlike the childhood story of the Sun and the Wind. The Wind approaches the Sun and suggests a competition to see which of them is the more powerful. The Wind points out a man standing below wearing a coat, and suggests that the strongest should surely be able to get the man to remove his coat. The Wind tries first, but the harder it blows the more the man clings onto his coat. The Wind eventually withdraws, exhausted, thinking that it will be impossible for the Sun to get the man to remove his coat. The Sun then says 'I'll try', and simply does nothing but shine, easily and effortlessly. Of course, to the Winds astonishment the man removes his coat.

The message is simple: Sometimes when we try too hard we can make a situation worse.

### So what can you do?

The first issue that we will need to address is how you react to your own painful feelings. To watch someone you love suffering with depression feels incredibly painful and may well provoke fear in you. Our natural inclination when we experience pain is to try to get rid of it. This presents a dilemma, because in trying to get rid of our pain, we can resort to using strategies that result in our loved one's situation becoming worse, as shown in Traps 1-7.

If you learn how to respond well to your own feelings, you can help your loved one respond well to theirs

The first step you need to take is to improve awareness of your own feelings. When you have decided it is OK for you to feel the way that you do, you will then feel under less pressure to resolve your loved one's situation. As a result of this any tension that you may feel will begin to lift. This is a very important strategy for you to master, because when you feel under less pressure, the pressure will also lift from your loved one.

### Tell your loved one that it is OK for him or her to feel the way that they do

Many of us feel that if we allow pain to be there, in this case the pain of low mood, it will get worse, and spiral out of control. We do not stop to think about trying such a radical strategy as approaching it.

### Help your loved one to come to you

As identified in the Traps section of this chapter, attempting to speed up the process of your loved ones movement out of a depressed state, by trying too hard, can have negative results.

Instead you will need to concentrate on creating a relaxed and more accepting atmosphere, so that your loved one will be more likely to turn to you to talk about what is troubling him/her. Individuals, vulnerable to becoming depressed are much more likely to talk openly to others who they believe will be accepting and non-judgemental of them.

### Key issues to be aware of when your loved one comes to you

You will need to listen without providing solutions and explain to your loved one that it is really OK for him/her to feel the way he/she does. Tell your loved one that anyone who has similar problems or similar thoughts would feel the same way he/she does. If your loved one comes up with his/her own solutions you need to encourage him/her, without suggesting any improvements that might come to mind.

You will also need to bear in mind that if you fall into any of the traps mentioned earlier, that any productive or helpful conversation could come to a very speedy end.

### How to respond to thinking errors that many individuals with depression have

Individuals who are vulnerable to becoming depressed are likely to think in an "all or nothing way" when they are experiencing depression. They may even say things such as "it is always going to be this way" "...all of the time ..." "nothing ever works out ..." and we rarely hear the words "sometimes" or "occasionally". It is important here that you do not come up with alternative evidence or argue against his/her position, as this can have the unfortunate consequence of keeping rigid thinking styles in place. Instead you will need to say things such as "I know that you feel this way right now. Even though you don't believe it right now, things will change, things will get better."

### How to help your child when they have low mood or if they are experiencing depression

Watching your child suffer with depression can induce considerable fear. The press frequently publish reports about individuals who have taken their own lives. There is no more awful a thought for parents than their child killing him/herself. Many of us take action (i.e., helping our children) to decrease our fear - often falling into the traps already outlined. If you take this type of action you will be perceived as controlling by your child, which ultimately can contribute to, and exacerbate his/her problems.

Parents are more likely to fall into traps than any other group of people who come into contact with individuals experiencing depression. With two concerned parents trying to help there is an even greater chance for traps to be activated. There can also be other problematic knock-on effects when siblings become involved.

As a parent, a major issue that you have to deal with is responsibility, and that somehow, and in some way, you are responsible for how your child is feeling. This could result in you trying too hard to fix the problem for your child.

You are naturally likely to be inclined to want to question your child about how and why he/she is feeling the way he/she is, because you want to help him/her resolve his/her difficulties. Such questions can be particularly difficult for young people to address.

So a general rule of thumb to bear in mind is to avoid at all costs falling into Traps 1 to 7.

---

**Here are examples of what you can do.**

- Ask no questions (e.g., "What's wrong?" "What's the matter?") Instead tell your son or daughter that if he/she wants someone to talk to, that you will be there for them.

- Concentrate on creating an environment that makes it easier for him/her to approach you.

- Be non-judgemental and use praise. Instead of trying to rationalise his/her feelings away, let him/her know that it is OK to feel the way that he/she does. If your child is a young adult, explain to him/her that the way he/she feels (while unpleasant) is normal, and is often part of growing up. Offer no solutions unless they are asked for. If they are young adults, tell them that low feelings, although unpleasant something that our body produces to help us.

- Approach your child, even if they push you away. Let them know that you are there for them. Praise them for all of their good points and tell them how much you love them. View yourself as being there to help, not to control. Let your child know that his/her feelings are accepted.

As parents we can have much more influence than we realise. Sometimes we don't tell our children how much we love them. Sometimes we don't apologise for things that we have done wrong, or for mistakes we have made in the past. Letting our children know that we have made errors is very important, as many children often blame themselves needlessly for things that were not their fault.

It is important that you do not seek forgiveness as your child may well try to minimise issues to protect you and they may say things such as "don't worry about it, it was nothing."

Many things that cause pain are not forgotten, even if they happened several years, even decades before. It is never too late to say sorry.

---

**How do you react to your feelings when your child tell you things about yourself that you don't want to hear?**

It is important to listen to your child and to let him/her speak. Sometimes he/she will say things that may be painful to hear, and when this occurs it is easy to get drawn into a defensive position. If this occurs, you need to encourage yourself to acknowledge your own feelings and resist the urge to defend yourself. If you do this, you will be carrying out excellent parenting behaviour. You will be showing your child how to accept responsibility by direct modelling and demonstration. In this case, actions definitely speak louder than words!

Even though you love your child you will need to remind yourself that he/she cannot read your mind

If you find it hard to express yourself to your child, it can be very helpful to write him/her a letter telling him/her all the things that you like and love about him/her and letting him/her know how you feel about him/her. You will need to choose your compliments very carefully, without criticism and - very importantly - without trying to teach.

If your child has made mistakes, which he/she regrets, you can remind him/her that it is very helpful to make mistakes as this is how we all grow and develop.

Finally, as a parent you are one of the most important role models in your child's life. Do not under any circumstances underestimate how important you are to them.

## Coping with a partner with depression

If your partner is suffering with depression, then there is little you can do to avoid it. It will impact on you as well.

Most people who are depressed find reading difficult. You can increase his/her motivation by doing things with him/her such as reading this book. People who are vulnerable to depression feel less alone if their partners take part in their recovery. Consider it a joint project!

For many individuals who experience depression there is a shift in their libido. Anti-depressants can also have a negative impact on sexual interest. If your partner does not want to have sex, you will need to remind yourself that it does not necessarily mean anything about you. If you believe that your partner's lack of interest in sex is about you, then you may feel rejected and you may engage in behaviours that will not help your partner's mood.

Depression can also affect your partner's ability to complete usual activities that previously would have been no problem. As suggested in the traps section, showing disapproval of his/her behaviour is unlikely to help lift him/her out of a depressed state.

### Specific behaviours to avoid if your partner is experiencing depression

- Flirting with other individuals
- Threatening to leave your partner
- Comparing your partner to previous partners
- Looking upon your partner as lazy, and selfish
- Being cross or angry with his/her mood
- Keeping his/her experience of depression a big secret

- Dropping your own interests and hobbies

---

**Important things that you we can do to help your partner**

- Let him/her know that it's OK for him/her to feel the way that he/she does.

- If children are involved, tell them what an important figure he/she is in his/her children's lives.

- Tell him/her all the things that you love and appreciate about him/her and feel grateful for about him/her.

- Encourage and support him/her to carry out activities, where results can be achieved very quickly with little effort e.g., short walks, eating small amounts, being around others, and having short conversations.

- Acknowledge his/her achievements, making it clear that you know that they might not see things as achievements because these were all things he/she could do before without much effort. A major problem that keeps people depressed is focussing on what they used to do and then telling themselves off for not being able to do it when they are experiencing depression. All this tends to do is to keep them stuck.

- Tell him/her that you understand that he/she is not where he/she wants to be yet, but that it's about getting there a bit at a time. Remind him/her of the question "How do you eat an elephant?" Answer – "One bite at a time"

- Remind him/her about how common depression is, that it is normal, and what is more important is how it is reacted to.

- When your partner is depressed, it is important to be tactile. But as already mentioned his/her libido is likely to be depressed as well. So when you are being tactile with your partner we need to touch him/her in a non-sexual way (e.g., touching his/her face, feet, arms, back, hair etc). He/she needs to be free from any illusion that we might want them to 'perform' sexually.

If, as a partner, you feel angry, irritated or resentful about following any of the above advice, then it may be that your relationship with your loved one is a factor in his/her symptoms of depression. It is not unusual for this to occur. However, it is important to be aware of it and to acknowledge it as a problem in its own right, and then take steps to address it together.